9 Timeless Nuggets

T0166917

9 Timeless Nuggets

Essential Marketing for the Young and Ambitious

BHARAT BAMBAWALE

PORTFOLIO
PENGUIN

An imprint of Penguin Random House

PORTFOLIO

USA | Canada | UK | Ireland | Australia
New Zealand | India | South Africa | China

Portfolio is part of the Penguin Random House group of companies
whose addresses can be found at global.penguinrandomhouse.com

Published by Penguin Random House India Pvt. Ltd
7th Floor, Infinity Tower C, DLF Cyber City,
Gurgaon 122 002, Haryana, India

Penguin
Random House
India

First published in Portfolio by Penguin Random House India 2020

Copyright © Bharat Bambawale 2020

All rights reserved

10 9 8 7 6 5 4 3 2

The views and opinions expressed in this book are the author's own and the
facts are as reported by him which have been verified to the extent possible,
and the publishers are not in any way liable for the same.

ISBN 9780670093854

Typeset in Minion Pro by Manipal Technologies Limited, Manipal
Printed at Replika Press Pvt. Ltd, India

This book is sold subject to the condition that it shall not, by way of trade
or otherwise, be lent, resold, hired out, or otherwise circulated without the
publisher's prior consent in any form of binding or cover other than that in
which it is published and without a similar condition including this condition
being imposed on the subsequent purchaser.

www.penguin.co.in

MIX
Paper from
responsible sources
FSC® C016779

I dedicate this book to my workplace mentors, especially those in the early years of my career, who taught me so many things that set me up for the road

Contents

Introduction

What this book will give you

As a young and ambitious marketer, you are looking for every advantage to kick-start your career.

You want to succeed, become an expert in your field, make a mark. In the script of your life that you write in your imagination, you see yourself doing amazing things: walking brave new paths, being clever and audacious, becoming a marketing great.

And yet, not everyone gets to the top. This is rarely because they don't have the desire, the energy, the discipline and the capacity for hard work. Most do. Often, it is because they don't get the right foundation, the coaching and the impetus to lift their career at the very outset.

I believe every young marketer like you has a shot at becoming a marketing great, for inside every young marketer is a craftsman, an artist, a pioneer. But finding and releasing that latent specialness in you requires that you get your marketing basics right and that you get a fair and equitable starting point to your career.

I wrote *Nine Timeless Nuggets* to provide you with a 2020 handbook of timeless marketing ideas, which will not only put you on an equal footing with others at the starting blocks but will also serve as a platform to help launch your career into the success stratosphere.

In these pages, you will find some fundamental ideas and concepts that have shaped my approach to marketing for over thirty-five years. I have written this book for students and new graduates of marketing, and for those in the first decade of their careers. Experienced marketers will find the ideas in this book familiar and should enjoy my fresh take on some of marketing's first principles.

To be a great marketer, you need to be a strategist and a tactician, someone who both thinks and does. In its simplest definition, marketing strategy is a road map for action; it defines the overall mission, vision and direction for marketing. Strategy, in short, bridges the gap between 'where we are' and 'where we want to be'. Marketing strategy brings value to the firm's overall business strategy by aligning business objectives with human behaviour. Ultimately, marketing is about people—about understanding what makes them think and do things. Marketing creates an environment around people, so that their thoughts and actions are beneficial to a brand. Conceptually, nothing can be simpler, right? And yet, many of the young marketers I come into contact with, accomplished tacticians though they are, ask me for guidance on the strategy side of our profession, which shows that their development needs aren't being met in that area.

'Why is this so?' you might ask. In no particular order, I see five reasons:

Too many students, too few teachers/mentors
Advertising's self-harming skill amputation
Debilitating invasion of foreign brands
The mixed blessing of technology
The demise of 'permission to fail'

1. Too many students, too few teachers/mentors

In the last quarter of a century, India's economy has grown in leaps and bounds. Domestic companies have expanded rapidly. New overseas companies have made investments here or have moved onshore. India's workforce hasn't been able to satiate the hunger for high-performance people at every level of management. The competition for human capital has intensified. Among the many strategies corporations adopt in the battle for talent, a time-tested and attractive one is to hire fresh graduates and 'home-grow' them. Traditional talent providers, like the IIMs and other well-known institutions, couldn't cater to the demand for B-schools, despite having opened new campuses in new cities. So edupreneurs jumped in to make up for the shortfall, and India has seen a tsunami of B-schools, not just in long-established university towns but also in small towns and semi-rural areas. These new places of learning also have to contend with India's human resource shortfalls, specifically in terms of finding, hiring and retaining great teachers of marketing. Small-town

B-schools are not generally abundant in teaching talent and make do with the teachers they can attract and keep, not the ones they aspire to.

The outcome is that fresh graduates joining companies are less prepared for the rigours of on-the-job marketing, despite their own and their B-school's best efforts.

A less-than-ideal academic background can be offset by on-the-job training and mentoring. Many companies have twelve- to eighteen-month training programmes. Thereafter, enhancements in marketing expertise come largely through experience and through coaching by workplace bosses and mentors. If these mentors are from backgrounds similar to those of the new employees, mentoring may fail to fill the fundamental knowledge deficit. With the demand for high-performance talent pulling the better managers rapidly up the hierarchy, there just aren't enough good mentors available. Besides, mentoring is a skill not every successful manager is good at.

2. Advertising agencies' self-harming skill amputation

In the '70s, and even the '80s and '90s, advertising agencies housed an admirable range of marketing skills. Agencies had client leaders (also called account managers), communication planners, media planners and buyers, researchers, graphic artists, TV and print producers, art directors, copywriters, photographers and so on. All were experts in their individual fields. Many had formidable reputations, earned through brilliance and hard work, that towered over the industry and its clients.

Agencies provided a range of services. They advised clients on their marketing strategy. They provided frameworks and research-based rationale for evaluating media. They designed and produced packaging, posters, TV ads, print ads, billboards, in-store displays, videos and sales conference material. Advertising agencies were highly valued partners for clients. The better agencies were fought over by competing clients. Many a client had spent time at an agency and many an agency person had been a client. People moving in either direction acknowledged they had developed their marketing skills at advertising agencies.

The first self-inflicted amputation agencies underwent started in the late '80s and was complete in a decade: Media planning and buying was hived off into a separate business from the main advertising agency, as were photography, packaging design, in-store displays and sales conference management. Gradually, over time, all that an agency was left with was TV and print creativity.

This not only depleted agencies of a range of vital marketing skills, it also laid the ground for a new kind of head of agency. Creative directors aspired, and ascended, to the chairman's office; by the 2000s, pretty much every advertising agency in India had promoted its creative director to chairman. Unsurprisingly, agencies started to privilege creativity over everything else, and soon most agency payrolls were made up largely of people who could write and produce TV and print ads.

As a consequence of this amputation, by the 2000s agencies were no longer repositories of a full range of marketing skills. They were print and TV advertising producers. More to the point, agencies were no longer equipped to give young entrants an all-round marketing education.

The second self-inflicted amputation was an outcome of the first. It was less the hacking of a limb than a deliberate deprivation of sustenance to a vital part of the body, making it wither. Under the regime of creative chairmen, an agency's client leader, who had formerly performed a vital central role in all the agency's interactions with clients, had his role pruned from one of fundamental importance to that of a process manager. While this might have seemed appropriate in the context of the creative chairman's goals for the agency, it had far-reaching consequences for advertising agencies.

If there was one person in an agency who knew the client's business in all its many complexities, for all its many challenges, and who partnered with clients through every step of their marketing journey, it was the client leader. Her marketing expertise was second to none. She knew the client's brand as well as, sometimes better than, the client's own team. She could strategize responses to a diverse range of marketing challenges better than any other person at the agency. She was the foremost marketing resource at the agency, and she taught and mentored fresh graduates in the principles and practices of marketing. When the writing on the wall for client leaders under creative chairmen became clear, the best ones departed to start their own agencies or consultancies.

The agencies they left may have thought this of little consequence, until another, perhaps unanticipated, outcome manifested: advertising agencies lost their long-standing invitation to the C-suite. In days gone by, corporate CEOs set store by the advice of client leaders because they were men and women of great wisdom and brought broad-spectrum marketing experience to the table. When agencies repositioned themselves as creative 'hot shops', trading mostly in TV and print ads, and with little marketing perspective to offer to clients, CEOs began to find less value in spending time with their agencies. CEOs were also facing challenges that even the best creative talent could not help them with: new types of competition and the advent of digital technology.

What this means in the context of this book is that whereas in the past young people had advertising agencies to learn marketing at, now they don't. Today's advertising agencies contribute only to a very small portion of the client's marketing blueprint.

3. The debilitating invasion of foreign brands

Historically, multinational corporations (MNCs) and their brands were viewed with well-deserved reverence in India. Hindustan Lever (now Hindustan Unilever Limited), Richardson Hindustan (now Procter & Gamble Company), Nestlé, SmithKline Beecham (now GlaxoSmithKline) and other giants were regarded as 'the real universities of marketing', where young graduates of merit could learn their marketing, earn their stripes and become big hitters. The admiration for these companies was inspired by a dual competence: they had, on the one hand, a bulging international playbook of best practices from around the world, while on the other hand they were inventing their own playbook of marketing for India. Young marketers could hone their craft using both these influences. Unsurprisingly, finding a placement at Hindustan Lever or Richardson Hindustan was every young marketer's dream. These companies did right by their young wards: they taught them, tested them and trusted them in positions of authority. The MNCs of yesteryear contributed literally hundreds of stars to Indian marketing—directly or through their associates.

But the companies that have come to our shores over the past twenty-odd years aren't like the MNCs of yesteryear. Walmart, Amazon, Samsung, Hyundai, Zara and Vodafone are just a few international brands that arrived in India during this time. Their technology is developed in another part of the world. Their products are developed in another part of the world. Their leaders live in another part of the world and only visit India as the need arises. The majority of these brands implement global strategies in India. Some localize advertising, but pretty much everything else is driven by global teams based elsewhere.

Even some international brands, with a long heritage in India and a considerable understanding of Indian ethos, such as Unilever's Lifebuoy, Surf and Lux, have undergone organizational changes. Today, Surf, Lifebuoy and Lux, for example, are controlled by offshore global teams. What is true of Hindustan Unilever Limited, which ceded brand leadership to global teams two decades ago, is true of other multinationals as well. Many of the multinationals India revered as 'the real universities of marketing' are no longer present in that avatar.

The debilitating impact of international brands running their marketing from foreign cities is this: it curtails the learning and growth of Indian talent. Our bright apprentices go from being thinkers to becoming doers, executors of directions their parent companies give them. MNCs aren't any more the places where young Indian talent can learn marketing fundamentals, as they did in the past.

4. The mixed blessing of technology

The penetration of mobile technology is likely to be 100 per cent among young Indian marketers (it will be close to that among all marketers, regardless of age). The mobile phone is the primary screen young marketers use, after which are the laptop and desktop. To search for information, the first door they knock is Google. Most will choose an information source from the first five listings. Few, if any, will look past the first page.

This is the first impact of technology: the search for information is becoming unidimensional, just as information itself has become more abundant than ever before. Interesting paradox, that.

The second is that the work-play boundary, once an unclimbable wall, has come down so low it is easily stepped over. Work and play coexist comfortably, and many are not aware which side of the wall they are on at any point in time. Most of us will divert from a work task to read and respond on Twitter, Facebook, YouTube, WhatsApp and other social media apps. We will book a flight, order lunch, buy a movie ticket, accept a date and arrange delivery of a new outfit. Few of us are able to remain continuously absorbed in a task for long stretches of time, even if the task demands it.

While it is fair to say that such behaviour is likely to be common among young marketers, it isn't predominant only among them. Even older marketers behave similarly, if in different proportions. But this behaviour shouldn't be deplored or criticized, though some might do that. It is to be accepted as the present-day context in which marketing strategy is created.

The third impact of technology has to do with the shortening of attention spans. Marketers tend not to read the 100-page report; they want the management summary. Better still, the summary of the summary, and best of all, the tweet. Information is being consumed in smaller and smaller packets. The smaller the packet, the less we know about a topic; and the less we know of the topic, the less craft we can bring to strategy. Over time, and this might be as short a period as a year or two, we *won't know what we don't know*. 'Strategy' will be built on small fragments of human understanding, leading to coarser starting points and less sophisticated output.

A few years ago, I was invited to consult for an Indian mobile phone brand. They sold several hundred thousand made-in-China, branded-in-India handsets annually. At my first meeting, I asked the marketing team a question, 'Who buys your brand?' I was looking for a description of their current customer. To my amazement, they couldn't answer me. The next question I asked was, 'Why do the people who buy your brand do so?' To my continued amazement, they did not know why. I was about to ask a third question but refrained from doing that, realizing I was embarrassing my hosts. My unasked question was this: 'If those who bought your brand were not to do so, which brands would they buy?' I wouldn't have been surprised if that question, too, went unanswered. The brand I refer to is, unsurprisingly, no longer in the mobile handset business.

I spent some time thinking about why that brand team was so poorly informed about their own brand. It struck me that the young guns on the brand had no framework to think about these issues. They did not know what to look for, which questions to ask. Small wonder then, that when hard days came along the brand had to shut that line of business.

5. The demise of 'permission to fail'

There was a time when in most companies trying something new was not just allowed, it was encouraged. Experimentation was a sign that you were looking for different ways in which to tackle a challenge. It was a badge of honour. Owners took pride in running companies where people chose to work because their corporate culture encouraged experimentation and learning.

Experimentation thrives in companies where people are not afraid to fail, indeed where people expect to fail from time to time. In such companies, failure does not signify a lack of intellect, rigour and discipline. It does not invite censure or ridicule, and does not derail careers. Instead, it simply leads one to the acknowledgement that in the exploration of all possible answers to a set of questions a business asks, some answers prove to be infeasible or suboptimal. Permission to fail is not about irresponsible licence; it is about disciplined experiments in search of better answers.

From Independence into the 1990s, pretty much everything in domestic marketing was being discovered. Whether MNC or Indian firm, finding new answers was the mantra and permission to fail was bestowed from the top, on the entire company, across departments and on all levels of hierarchy. There was a boldness, a hunger for discovery, which infused and enthused everyone and everything including marketing. After the 1990s, just as Indian businesses started to grow through economic liberalization, Indian marketing started becoming risk-averse even as the stakes rose. Quick return on investment became the only goal, and the first casualty was permission to fail.

This state of affairs, which defines contemporary businesses, is aggravated by quarterly results announcements: if a company has a few successive bad quarters, their stock prices tumble and CEOs are immediately under pressure. When bottom lines need shoring up, the axe first falls on marketing budgets. Only the most obvious and tried-and-tested methods and practices escape the cut.

Everybody—including young marketers—learns when they are free of the fear of failure. You learn by trying; you learn by finding out why some ideas work and others don't. When the money men pull the plug, a company's performance looks better in the short term. The longer-term damage to what that company knows, and what it does better than others, is not immediately seen. But the damage does take place—sometimes irreparably so. The continuously experimenting company is a better long-term investment than the budget-cutter. It attracts better people, has a better culture, makes better products, markets them better and prospers for longer.

As a consequence of the withdrawal of permission to fail in post-1990s India, a crucial workplace avenue to marketing learning was curtailed. Obviously, young marketers do get better at some things but those aren't always connected to the originality and inventiveness that brilliant marketing requires.

Nine Timeless Nuggets is arranged in three sections, with three chapters each. In every chapter, there's at least one powerful model you can use.

Section 1: How to Think of People

Chapter 1: Who Are We Talking To?
Nugget 1: The Multi-identity Customer Is Now Mainstream

Chapter 2: Why Do People Buy?
Nugget 2: A New Customer Motivation Model

Chapter 3: How Do We Influence People?
Nugget 3: Uses of the Customer Motivation Model

Section 2: How to Craft Your Brand

Chapter 4: Where Do Brands Come From?
Nugget 4: Learning from the Past to Shape Tomorrow's Brands

Chapter 5: How Did Brands Get Here?
Nugget 5: Brand Octagon Model for the Twenty-First-Century Brand

Nine Timeless Nuggets is here to give you a launching pad from where to soar. I hope it will be the wind under your wings. I hope it will help you realize your ambition to become one of India's marketing greats.

Section 1

How to Think of People

I

Who Are We Talking To?

Nugget 1: The Multi-Identity Customer Is Now Mainstream

'. . . [B]ut it's no use going back to yesterday, because I was a different person then.'

—Alice in Lewis Carroll's *Alice's Adventures in Wonderland*

In M. Night Shyamalan's 2016 movie *Split*, actor James McAvoy plays a character in whom twenty-three identities live. They range from docile to guileful to malevolent. The struggle for dominance between them is a continuing battle; when the more sinister ones take over, there are terrifying consequences. The possessor of these identities is part saint, part sinner, sometimes effusive and charming, at others cunning and murderous, with one section of his mind anchored in reality, the other delusional.

Split is not the first movie on the subject. Hollywood has long been drawn to the storytelling possibilities of dissociated identities, producing at least thirty-five films about the condition in the last fifty years. Hollywood has given us *Dr. Jekyll and Mr. Hyde*, based on a tale that has seen multiple screen presentations, as well as *Fight Club, Psycho, Me, Myself & Irene, Dressed to Kill* and *The Machinist* among many others. Central to each story is a character heroically transformed—or tragically torn apart—by multiple personalities. The lead character's transformation is sometimes amusing and appealing, sometimes bizarre and revolting. The character always struggles to come to terms with what is happening to him and often tries to subdue the other 'person' inside. More often than not the struggle—whether within oneself or with forces outside—is extremely difficult, destructive, even fatal.

From a medical or movie point of view, multiple personality disorder, like many an illness, is a problem that affects few individuals. They can be identified, contained if not quarantined, and treated. It is not a problem of the population at large. The mainstream continues to be 'normal', each with a single, well-understood and predictable identity. This, the underlying belief seems to be, is desirable and good for relationships. Multiple identities inside one person, however benign they may be, make relationships unpredictable, difficult to manage and eventually doomed to fail.

But what if having multiple personalities is not a *disorder* but rather the *true order* of humanity? It is not an aberration and it is not rare; it is normal and describes each and every one of us. It is not a condition; it is a way of life. It does not destroy; it shapes who we are. It is not something to be isolated and treated; it should be embraced, even celebrated. It is the new consumer paradigm that will drive businesses in the future and create never-before-seen opportunities—and challenges—for marketers.

Welcome to a world of *individual multitude* that is turning long-prevailing models of the needs hierarchy on their heads. Welcome to the next phase of marketing, where brands will not only no longer have the comfort of marketing to large, homogeneous groups of consumers but will have to market to millions of individuals with multiple personalities having concurrent, often contradictory needs.

How did we get here?

Simplistic as it sounds, how people behave depends on who they are and what stimuli they receive from their surroundings. Over a period of time, both people and surroundings influence and change each other. Science and intellect allow us to bring sophistication to the construct, but in its essence the construct is simple. In the same surroundings, two people might react very differently to one another on account of their personalities. Nelson Mandela emerged after twenty-seven years of incarceration with his dream of a truly democratic, apartheid-free South Africa intact and no rancour towards his captors. Another prisoner, with a personality different from Mandela's, undergoing an equally harsh imprisonment, might have stepped out with hatred in his heart and revenge on his mind. Conversely, the same person put in two very different surroundings might behave very differently. Following the 1991 break-up of the USSR, from the Yeltsin years through to the present times under Putin, Russians who were previously socialists have taken to a larger-than-life pursuit of wealth and hedonism. What changed? Not the people as much as the political ideology and system around them.

It is this basic understanding of who people are and how they behave that shapes most behavioural insights. It also gives us the basis of understanding India and the changes people are going through, both as citizens and as consumers. Diverse sets of people were united under one nation at Independence. Since then, India has seen far-reaching changes in ideology every twenty years or so, from democratic socialism to liberalization to our present-day consumerism. In an interesting contrast, we have undergone broad unifying changes at a national level while simultaneously liberating our individual identities.

At Independence, Indians were essentially of two types: those who were like the British and those who were not. The former group often had worked for the British, had exposure to their and other Westerners' lifestyles, spoke English, primarily wore Western attire, bought imported brands, studied at schools and colleges that were replicas of the British system and lived by the Gregorian calendar. The second type of Indians would have studied in Hindi or another Indian language, worn primarily Indian attire, might have participated in anti-British activities during the freedom struggle, preserved an Indian lifestyle and lived by the Indian lunar calendar. What unified both types of Indians were the call of the flag and the desire to build an independent, new nation.

Before and after Independence, India had a number of expatriates running the Indian branches of overseas companies. One such was Frank Gerard, who started the Indian operation of the American global advertising agency J. Walter Thompson (JWT). Another was Edward John ('Peter') Fielden, who served as chairman of JWT for thirty-six years. Vikram Doctor, in his 2004 article for the *Economic Times*, shines a light on that bygone period of Indian marketing. Of special interest is that many of JWT's accounts of that time, including General Motors, Chesebrough-Pond's, Vaseline, Elizabeth Arden and so on were, like JWT itself, the Indian operations of American and British firms. The clients Gerard and Fielden met were expatriates like themselves, their conversations were held in GM's vehicle assembly plant at Sewri in Central Bombay or similar client locations. What was true of JWT was also true of many other agencies and their clients.

If you went shopping at that time, you might well have visited the Army and Navy Store or put in an order for a Studebaker Champion sedan or a Lambretta scooter. You might have started your day with Colgate and Lux, have had Glaxo treat you when unwell and Horlicks revive you when convalescing, while you secretly lit an Imperial Tobacco cigarette against your doctor's advice. (As an aside, a Chevrolet sedan would have set you back Rs 3600 in 1927. In 1961 a Lambretta moped was Rs 790.) This is not to say you could not at the same time sip a Rooh Afza as you snacked on a Parle Gluco biscuit, or a Vadilal ice cream at one of their soda fountains, put your faith in a Doctor Burman ayurvedic treatment or operated an account with Allahabad Bank. You could indeed have done all that, as India offered both sets of brands to customers. That said—and perhaps on account of the lingering influence of the recently departed British, expatriates in corporate leadership, the Indian managers they trained and the aspiration for imported products—India's first post-Independence consumer identity had a distinct international flavour.

Marketing asks its practitioners to target a specific audience, and from the millions that comprise that audience to paint a picture of that one person the brand wants to speak to. A description of such a person, in the period from Independence to the end of the 1960s, would likely have read something like this: 'An Indian in his or her mid-twenties in Calcutta, New Delhi, Bombay and Madras; from an upper-class family; casually elegant in beautifully tailored suits; educated in English at an Indian public school and graduate of a prestigious college; now employed at a multinational firm or in the civil services; confident in fine dining, Western music and ballroom dancing; on the way up in life.'

In short, the first unified post-Independence Indian customer identity leaned towards the West in terms of aspiration and lifestyle. A 'babu' if you like, without the derogatory connotations of that term.

The fact that this way of life, and the means to afford and indulge it, was accessible to only a tiny minority of Indians was not lost on India's marketing and business leaders and even less so on the political leadership. If all Indians were to have a better life, the imperative was to drive the benefits of prosperity down the population pyramid. To achieve this, and concurrently address historical injustices to certain sections of Indian society, the leadership of that time embraced the idea of India as a socialist democracy. This led India, among other things, to building large, Russia-inspired steel plants and mini cities in Rourkela and Bokaro; setting up giant public-sector undertakings (PSUs) like the National Thermal Power Corporation Limited; issuing licences to control entrepreneurial adventure and quotas to equalize manufacturing opportunity to prevent one or two big players from dominating; and promoting cooperatives such as the Kaira District Cooperative Milk Producers' Union. The slogan *'Jai Jawan, Jai Kisan'* invited us to admire our soldiers and farmers. Agriculture was the chief source of national income, although more and more Indians were going to work, many of them in PSUs. Indians were far from wealthy, and a salary of Rs 1500 per month was considered generous.

Large private-sector groups, like Tata, Birla and Bajaj, set forth their templates for multi-industry growth. Multinationals like Unilever, Richardson Vicks and Nestlé took fresh guard and began playing their shots with new purpose, albeit tempered by a national policy prejudiced against overseas ownership. Despite this new energy, there was a perceptible entrepreneurial sobriety in the private sector, influenced by government policy and perhaps the Emergency of 1975. Government liaison—for the procurement of business licences, the negotiation of quotas and any other benefits, and allowances that could be brought the corporations' way—was a key contributor to competitiveness and success. The overriding business philosophy was to mass-manufacture acceptable-quality products and make them available at as low a price as possible—but only so much that your firm wouldn't be adversely noticed for its ambitions. Luxury was out of reach; those who flew Air India and were pampered by the Maharaja's glamorous flight attendants lived a life most Indians couldn't even dream of.

As incomes grew, so did demand. Demand that could not be met by supply lines frequently suppressed by factors like licences and quotas, a cautious approach towards investment and few competitors in each category. Indians who remember those days are wryly nostalgic about waiting for up to ten years for the delivery of a Bajaj scooter. Amul butter, which is ubiquitous today, faced frequent stock-outs. The Premier Padmini, now an amusing relic of times gone by, was an exciting new launch. The atmosphere was not one of abundance, and most Indians took a conservative approach to the future; even those with relatively low incomes found a way to save a little something as a buffer against hard times.

Despite these pressures, the 1970s and 1980s were a period of tremendous social osmosis. The identities, of those who had started out more like the British and of those who hadn't, began to merge, the demarcating lines began to blur. More people from diverse educational and social backgrounds joined the workforce; more people travelled to new cities in non-native states for their careers; Indians started to date and marry, albeit in tiny numbers, partners from other states and cultures. Indians one generation removed from the freedom struggle had no personal reference points in the past and no idea of what the future might hold. State-owned Doordarshan played a seminal role in shaping Indian life, first in the black-and-white days of the 1960s and 1970s, and later by ushering in the age of colour television in 1982. Doordarshan started to accept commercial advertising in 1984, creating massive viewership for shows like *Chitrahaar* and *Hum Log*, India's first blockbuster serial. Perhaps because of this, and despite Doordarshan's robust regional-language programming, Hindi started to become the lingua franca of business and, just a short step away, that of marketing and advertising. Indians responded with pride and pleasure to the nationalist undertones of Lintas' 'Hamara Bajaj' TV commercial and to the more obvious overtones of the national integration messages of 'Freedom Run: The Torch Song' and 'Mile Sur Mera Tumhara', created by Ogilvy & Mather's Suresh Mullick. It is this start that subsequent craftsmen such as Piyush Pandey of Ogilvy raised to popular heights with memorable marketing campaigns in Hindi. An unintended consequence was the demise of the primarily English-speaking marketer who had held sway in the previous decades.

And through all this, perhaps because of all this, a new customer identity was taking shape, one that was a hybrid of national and personal identities. Indians were buying TVS and Luna mopeds, while also welcoming sandwich spreads into their diets and chocolates as a way of expressing their feelings when words failed. India's entrepreneurs started to think beyond the constraints that had previously governed them. Bajaj's monopoly was challenged by the runaway success of Kinetic Honda, just as the monopoly of

Premier and Hindustan Motors (HM) was challenged by the triumphant Maruti Suzuki. Kinetic Honda and Maruti Suzuki were the emerging brands of that time: a combination of modern Western technology offered through an Indian partner, each imbuing the brand with their individual DNA, creating a value proposition that Indians found irresistible.

Through this evolved the second singular Indian customer identity: the 'hybrid'. A description of such a person would likely be, 'A married Indian in his or her early thirties, in the metros of Mumbai, Kolkata, Delhi or Chennai but also in mini metros such as Pune and Hyderabad; from a middle-class family; equally comfortable in Indian and Western attire; educated in tier-two schools; bi- or multi-lingual; upwardly mobile in a career with a multinational or Indian firm; likely to order kebabs and chaat at the British-legacy Gymkhana Club while comfortably conversing with an international visitor in English.'

By the end of the '80s, that generation of Indians had conclusively stepped out of the shadow of British times. The British presence in India was an era which provided a few chapters to high-school history books. A heady individualism was starting to bubble. It is these flames that economic liberalization fanned from the mid-1990s through to current times.

One of liberalization's impacts has been to drive the desire for upward mobility down into the lower levels of the Indian population pyramid. Education, technology, entrepreneurship, jobs, connectivity, travel—the traditional levers of success and individual enterprise—became available to more and more Indians in more and more parts of the country. The metros and mini metros absorbed millions of small-town and rural upward-mobility seekers and became mega cities. With liberalization, India shrugged off the last pretence of socialism as a guiding principle. Getting rich and living rich—and doing it on your own terms, with or without the approval of the authorities—became a strong vector for most Indians. We were still Indian, and national sentiment still glued us together (especially when India was playing international cricket), but under that overlay it was each man for himself. Soon, many more people were not just well off, they were wealthy. India's new first-generation wealthy declined the traditional attractions of sophistication and polish: as prosperity went down the population pyramid, a folksy culture bubbled up to become all-pervading in Indian life. This was aided by the privatization of TV channels. The scramble for television rating points to attract the advertiser's rupee led to an explosion of entertainment catering to the broadest of tastes. India was soon under an avalanche of *saas-bahu* serials, with costumes and sets in every colour of the rainbow, wild dancing to Bollywood-clone music and loud multi-day wedding galas. In-your-face hedonism in every segment of India's population became the order of the day.

This gives us the third singular Indian customer identity: the 'hedonist'. A description of such a person, or rather such a family, would likely be, 'An Indian family; parents in their mid-thirties with two or more children, in Delhi, Mumbai, Kolkata, Chennai, Pune and Hyderabad, but also in Indore, Nagpur, Varanasi, Vijayawada, Jaipur and smaller towns; primarily comfortable in Indian attire but wear some Western clothes; educated in schools of every kind; primarily conversing in Indian languages; wanting to get rich on their own steam; likely to enjoy bhangra remixes and street food; shop for home and personal items using TV shopping networks.'

Where do we go from here?

Even as the 'hedonist' is India's prevailing consumer avatar, a secret fragmentation is afoot, as a thousand tiny personal and social revolutions quietly play out. An admittedly small but now noticeable segment of well-qualified women in large cities are self-deterministic, eschewing traditional roles, living alone, prioritizing careers over motherhood, choosing divorce over marital unhappiness and personal fulfilment over self-sacrificing duty. E-commerce is changing the retail landscape. Fewer meals are being cooked at home as food delivery grows. The nuclear family is far from rare and is now seen even in small-town India. More Indians are finding their life partners across the fabric of society, not just from within their communities. Smartphones are changing the content Indians consume, and this is shaping new personas and life stories. Streaming services in entertainment are doing to private TV channels what the latter did to Doordarshan two decades ago. Data is telling us what people really want. Fissures and fault lines are appearing in what was, at least to the public eye, a homogeneous society. Indian and foreign brands vie side by side in the tumultuous Indian marketplace. The marketers' ideal of a single predictable identity is breaking down faster than ever under the influence of new technology and new life values. More to the point, Indians are changing—in some regards quietly and below the surface, while in others loudly and publicly.

The truth is that the Indian customer never had a single identity. We are a single nation, united by certain beliefs and principles, but under that we have always been, and continue to be, a patchwork quilt. The single-identity, single-personality Indian was a marketing convenience. It never actually was the truth about Indians, whether as people or as customers.

Under the meta-narrative of being Indian, a thousand micro-narratives swirl within each of us. If one Indian has been to the top schools and colleges and aspires to a frills-free life, another might have never seen a big city until landing his first job and is driven to be rich at any cost. Each story is different, with many hues, motivations and pay-offs. No customer is just one thing any more. Since marketing is principally about creating desired behaviour by managing the environment around people, marketers must contend with the challenge of knowing individuals, as well as the macro environment that is shaping them, better. How do you deal with complexity in people, shaped by complexity in environment, which in turn is being shaped by complexity in people?

Marketing to a single consumer identity is a thing of the past. Multiple-personality Indians are tearing the rule book of traditional models. Multiple needs, springing from multiple personalities, will coexist. This is the new Indian customer. This is the marketing territory of the future. If you are navigating this territory for brand and business success, you need a new marketing blueprint.

II

Why Do People Buy?

Nugget 2: A New Customer Motivation Model

'*Do I contradict myself? Very well then I contradict myself,*
(I am large, I contain multitudes.)'

—Walt Whitman, 'Song of Myself, 51'

It is a central purpose of marketers to get insights into what drives human behaviour. How do ideas take root? How do we make choices? What direct and indirect influences affect our choices? How can our investigations into human motivations be organized and brought into daily use? These are some of the questions marketers have sought the answers for, or better answers for, since the inception of marketing.

Surprisingly, the primary model for understanding human motivations remains one which began its development towards the end of World War II, despite the fact that it is more than half a century old and that our present-day concerns are enormously different and complex. This is Abraham Maslow's 'Hierarchy of Needs'. The model found widespread use and appreciation mid-'50s onwards, after the publication of Maslow's book *Motivation and Personality*. In his 'hierarchy', Maslow described five areas of human motivation, generally presented in the shape of a pyramid.

Maslow's model puts *biological and physiological needs* at the base of the pyramid. These are fundamental life needs, such as air, food, drink, shelter, warmth, sex and sleep; only when these are met, Maslow postulated, do humans start to be motivated by higher-order needs.

One rung up the hierarchy are *safety needs*, such as protection, security, law and order and stability. As India's rural population accelerates its migration into our already overstretched cities, there is unprecedented pressure on public services to cope.[1] Long-term residents of Indian cities bemoan the decay of public order, personal safety and civility. Security guards at entrances to houses and apartment complexes have been commonplace for years, as are security cameras in reception areas. The need for safety can create a range of behaviours and products: while India has taken a less aggressive approach, the United States of America, whose citizens have the right to bear arms, has seen a surge in gun sales.

The next tier in Maslow's pyramid contains *belongingness and love,* which include friendship, intimacy and familial ties.

---

[1]   According to a 2010 McKinsey Global Institute study, India's urban population will touch 590 million in 2030, a figure which, as a TERI report projects, will further rise to 814 million by 2050 (https://www.teriin.org/resilient-cities/urbanisation.php).

Their position on the pyramid suggests that only when we are well fed and safe do we look for mate selection, progeny and companionship. However, one look at the pavements in most Indian cities, or at the spaces underneath bridges and flyovers, throws this assertion into question. Here, large families of migrants, itinerants and the homeless live, cook, eat and have multiple children, with neither a roof over their heads nor any measure of personal safety. This suggests that the need for belongingness and love thrives even when food and safety are far from guaranteed.

Next up are *esteem needs*: respect, status, recognition and so on. These are stacked in the fourth tier, implying that we look for status and recognition only after all the needs in the three lower tiers are fulfilled. Yet, when we look at India's underprivileged sections of society, including castes and tribes that have suffered hundreds of years of prejudice and deprivation, we see that their present-day demands are not limited to food, clothing, safety and family; they demand concurrently respect and recognition, an equal place at the table and genuine opportunities in an advancing society. In other words, esteem needs are deeply intertwined with lower-order motivations, even when some of the lower-level needs are only partially fulfilled.

Topping the pyramid are *self-actualization needs*: the desire to be everything one can be. This includes self-expression as well as spiritualism and exploring higher consciousness. Its position at the apex of the pyramid rests on the belief that only when you have scaled the four lower levels will you reach for the topmost motivation. There is a measure of truth in this, offset only by those whose beliefs or convictions propel them towards self-actualization even without the consummation of lower-order needs. Monks in certain religious orders, as also the famous Warkaris of Maharashtra, who devote themselves to extreme voluntary frugality in the worship of Vithoba, an incarnation of Vishnu, are examples of this.

Most marketers discover Maslow's hierarchy as students. The model remains useful throughout their careers, as few other models make human motivations more systematic and easy to follow. However, despite its pre-eminence, does Maslow's hierarchy provide a contemporary framework for marketing, guiding us through how people's desire for products is built, why they buy things, how they value brands? Are human needs today akin to a sequential multi-course meal, as Maslow's model suggests, in which one course is consumed before the next is served? Or is need satisfaction today more accurately like a smorgasbord, with diners helping themselves to a buffet in any order they choose— even if dessert precedes soup.

Today, many a rural Indian teenager, with very little cash to spend, will happily forego a rarely affordable bar of chocolate, and even more readily a filling meal, to pay for a mobile Internet data plan. Urban twenty-somethings in romantic relationships are known to choose binge watching Netflix over intimacy. Voluntary sleep deprivation in favour of online gaming is well-documented. And some tech companies are advocating that Internet access be made a fundamental human right. In other words, the progressive neatness of Maslow's hierarchy has undergone an untidy scrambling in today's times.

My intention is not to cast any aspersion on Maslow's hierarchy, which continues to be influential and useful for anyone willing to develop a broad understanding of human motivations. My intention is to make a case for a more predictive model of customer motivation, which I shall introduce later in this chapter.

Curiously, there have been no viable alternatives to the Maslow model over the years. In 2015 the management consultancy firm Bain & Company introduced a model that has superficial similarities with Maslow's. The Bain & Co. model is also a pyramid and also works with the idea that higher-order gratifications sequentially follow lower-order ones. But that is where the similarity ends. The Bain & Co. 'Elements of Value' model intertwines needs, benefits and product features to define four levels of value: functional, emotional, life change and social impact. Bain & Co. used multiple data points from their research over the years to propose a different hierarchy, in which four levels hold a distribution of thirty elements of value that drive customer loyalty and revenue growth. At the base of the Bain & Co. pyramid sit *functional* elements of value, such as saving time, making money, reducing risk and organizing. In the tier above these sit *emotional* elements of value, such as nostalgia, design and aesthetics. The next tier houses *life-changing* elements, such as providing hope, affiliation and self-actualization. At the apex is *social impact*, where self-transcendent value is looked for.

The Bain & Co. model is a hybrid of needs, benefits and product features. Its largest apparent utility seems to be in product development, using one or more of the thirty value drivers. That leaves us with a question: Does Bain & Co.'s Elements of Value, a powerful tool though it is, concede valuable territory in the motivations area while stepping into the adjacent product development area? Do functional, emotional, life-changing and social-impact parameters adequately describe how humans, particularly we Indians, make choices today? Can our motivational framework be reduced to these four levels of value?

Moving on from 'first-this-then-that' progression models, like the two mentioned above, there are a few 'random' human motivation models, such as the one devised by the popular life coach Tony Robbins. The 'Six Core Human Needs' model by Robbins posits that our need for *certainty* (that we can avoid pain and attain pleasure while feeling safe, secure and comfortable) sits alongside our need for *variety* (physical and emotional challenge and surprise), *significance* (to feel needed, wanted and worthy), *love, connection, growth* (intellectual, emotional and spiritual) and *contribution* (to contribute to and support the lives of others). In one way, Robbins's model harks back to the 'purity' of Maslow's model, by touching on core human needs and drivers. That said, Robbins's model makes a noteworthy departure from Maslow's and Bain & Co.'s models: Robbins does not view human needs as a progression. His approach is in line with the idea that humans exhibit all six needs, all of the time. I imagine Robbins's followers, of whom I am not one, find great value and potential for personal growth in his model as well as in his seminars and life coaching. My reason for liking his model is this: Robbins underlines that humans *inhabit multiple need states simultaneously*, not sequentially, thereby disrupting the beguiling neatness and allure of hierarchy models.

This is my own central assertion about human motivation and relates to the idea of the multiple-identity customer in the previous chapter. Whereas progressive models are built on the premise that lower-order needs precede higher-order ones—a premise that might have held true at certain times in the past and in certain contexts—a more accurate description of today's human motivations is *simultaneous multiplicity*.

It is not my intention to criticize long-serving models or their authors, or to suggest that we discard one model for another. Every model is useful in its own way: a marketer's understanding of human motivations is sharpened and layered by looking at people through multiple lenses. The question I pose is this: Do past models describe customer motivations through a framework and in a language that genuinely reflect how people are today? Is there room for another model to understand people, one that is not just accurate but also predictive?

With this in mind, I developed my own customer motivation model, which I personally use when thinking of the question, 'Why do people buy?' I emphasize that my model is offered in the specific context of people as *customers*. There are, of course, other contexts, wherein other models might have more to offer.

Customer Motivation Model

INNER-DIRECTED MOTIVATORS	OUTER-DIRECTED MOTIVATORS
Good sense	One-upmanship
Self-love	FOMO
Hedonism	Attention
Joy of ownership	Connection
Personal reinvention	Vanity
Value-added experiences	Social credit
Private legacy	Public legacy

INFLUENCERS

Money   Values   Personality   Time

The model is a synthesis of my observations, learning and practice from over thirty-five years in marketing and advertising. It looks at people through the lens of *what makes us become customers*. All of us have two sets of motivators that propel our consumption behaviour. The first set includes *inner-directed motivators*: the things that drive us within ourselves, that make us what we are when no one else is watching, what we see in our inner mirror when we are completely transparent with ourselves, without disguise, delusion, adornment or illusion. The second set is dedicated to *outward-directed motivators*. These are also about us, of course, but pertain to what we are when we are with others, when we want something from others, when we are putting on a face, creating an image, investing in illusion and drawing attention to ourselves. Both sets of motivators intertwine with each other to lead us to the gratifications we seek in life. These gratifications can come from people, places or products. Or, more potently than products, from brands. Apart from the two sets of motivators, there is one more dimension to my customer motivation model: *influencers*, of which there are four. The first is *money*, or more precisely our spending power. The second is *values*, which is the moral framework we are brought up with and which guides our decision-making at a macro level. Third is *personality*, relating to the introversive and extroversive traits within us, which obviously impact our choices. Fourth and last is *time*, which plays a part in two ways: first, in terms of the short- and long-term scopes of our choices, and second, in terms of the moment of time in our life when we are making a particular choice.

Aspects of the customer motivation model

1. It is a 'simultaneous multiplicity' model. It rests on the conviction that most, if not all, motivations that spring up within us are concurrently active.
2. The motivators are not ranked. In putting *good sense* first on the inner-directed motivators list and *one-upmanship* first on the outer-directed list, I don't intend to imply that these two are more important than the others.
3. Motivations overlap, are intertwined with each other and work in tandem. The need for *attention* might express alongside *joy of ownership* in one customer and alongside *good sense* in another. Look at motorcycle enthusiasts. *Attention* combined with *joy of ownership* might lead

one customer to a Harley-Davidson Fat Boy. The same
motivator—*attention*—combined with *good sense* might
take another customer to a Bajaj Pulsar. Both brands fulfil
the attention need, with the second motivator pulling
each customer towards a different brand choice.

4. There is no barrier separating inner-directed motivators
   from outer-directed ones. Motivators are fluid and
   combine harmoniously with each other (for the most
   part). Inner-directed motivators are symbiotic with other
   inner-directed motivators as well as with outer-directed
   motivators.

5. Some motivations combine well with others to form
   motivator pairs or trios. For example, *vanity* and
   hedonism might act together to lead a customer to a
   Sabyasachi or Tahiliani outfit for a special occasion, like
   a wedding reception or a fashion show. But on other days
   vanity might be tempered by *good sense*, leading the same
   customer to everyday fashion from Zara or H&M. As is
   evident, customers seek a range of gratifications even
   within a category, depending on which motivators pair
   with which other ones.

6. The relationships between motivators are not permanent
   or hardwired. Motivators form short- and long-term fits
   with each other. Think of this as a dynamic, perpetual-
   motion, three-dimensional machine, made up of a
   number of different-sized gear wheels. Each wheel
   corresponds to a motivator. The relative sizes of the wheels
   correspond to the sizes of motivators at various points
   in time. Some wheels are small, some are big. Some big
   wheels temporarily shrink, others grow larger. And then

this changes all over again. This motivations machine that lies inside each of us is in continuous, churning motion, with the teeth of each gear wheel locking with and unlocking from the teeth of other wheels, producing endless combinations of gratification-seeking needs and motivations.

Let's look at how the model works in relationship to products and brands. We can use toothpaste as our first example. Mundane perhaps, but something we all need throughout our lives. How do we choose one toothpaste over the other? For a child, we might look for cavity protection as children's teeth are prone to decay. In early and mid-adulthood, we might choose one that promises fresh breath, since we expect to be close to others. As seniors, we might opt for a sensitive toothpaste, which helps buffer our teeth from the darts of pain due to depleted enamel. Regardless of which choice we make, we do so because something makes sense to us in a life stage and solves a problem. A toothpaste is therefore, after all is said and done, primarily a *good sense* purchase, with aspects like practicality, convenience and financial value rolled into it. But toothpaste purchase isn't only good sense. The added promise of white teeth might also appeal to our needs for *attention* and *vanity*. Strong teeth that belie our age might also satisfy our needs for *social credit* and *one-upmanship*. Even in an everyday category like toothpaste, we see the interlocking of multiple motivators. This is where brands come into play: by understanding that motivators form pairs and trios, and designing gratifications that meet nuanced combinations of these, brands make themselves vital to people in creating real-life outcomes. But more on this later in the book.

Let's look at another example. Avanti, a young woman in her early twenties, completes her master's degree and moves from Nagpur to Mumbai for her first job. She will look for a range of products and services as she settles into Mumbai, based on a range of needs and motivators. Let's focus on just one—*connection*. One expression of the *connection* motivator is *companionship*. As a new arrival in Mumbai, Avanti will want to make friends. Her initial channels for finding friends are work, other friends and social media. She will meet people at Café Coffee Day, book restaurants through Zomato, spend many a long evening at Social and order home delivery on Swiggy for a rare night in. As time passes, Avanti feels settled in Mumbai. She has a stable set of friends and a comfortable set of activities to perform. She is more assured and assertive socially and at work. A question strikes her: Am I doing the things long-term Mumbai residents do? Or are there hidden subcultures that I neither see nor experience? Avanti's *FOMO* (fear of missing out) motivator has come into play, and soon her exploration entails asking long-term Mumbaikars she knows questions about the city, trawling social media and checking out websites for hidden gems. Alongside *FOMO*, her *value-added experiences* motivator is also hyperactive and her choices spring from an interweaving of three motivators: *connection*, *FOMO* and *value-added experiences*. More time passes and another facet of Avanti's *connection* motivator finds expression and urgency—love and romance. This will get her to frequently swipe left on Tinder, and occasionally right, as she explores the ups and downs of dating. Dating might require some *personal reinvention*, possibly pushing her in the direction of Gold's Gym, BBlunt and Nicobar. It will also call for *social credit*, as garnered through the confident use of cutlery, a preference in wine and an open mind for unfamiliar cuisines. Might dating an attractive partner also have sprinkles of *vanity* and *one-upmanship*?

This brief glimpse into Avanti's life underlines the complexity, concurrency and continuity of human needs and motivators, and how the intertwining of these motivators leads us to a variety of brands, products and services.

A question on some minds might be this: Can a motivation model really be that simple? Can it be reduced to just fourteen motivators? Aren't there various dimensions to each of the fourteen motivators? Those are excellent questions, to which the answers are, yes, yes and yes. Yes, while the model is simple, it covers the human drivers; and yes, there are dimensions to each motivator. Each motivator has one or more sub-motivators. *Good sense* has aspects of pragmatism, financial astuteness and convenience. *Self-love* includes the need for food, shelter and security. Sensual gratification, non-reproductive sex and various kinds of excesses are dimensions of *hedonism*. *Attention* contains the wish to attract others, stand out and be appreciated. *Vanity* is about pride, admiration and having a following.

Now let's look at the four influencers—money, values, personality and time—one by one. Each influencer plays a role in the interpretation of motivators. Let's go back to Avanti to explore them.

Customer Motivation Model: Sub-motivators

INNER-DIRECTED MOTIVATORS	OUTER-DIRECTED MOTIVATORS
Good sense (pragmatism, financial astuteness, convenience)	**One-upmanship** (competition, victory, advancement)
Self-love (food, shelter, security)	**FOMO** (belonging, equality, excitement)
Hedonism (sensual gratification, sex, excess)	**Attention** (attraction, standing out, appreciation)
Joy of ownership (possessiveness, attachment, play)	**Connection** (significant others, family, friends, interest groups)
Personal reinvention (nurture>nature, escape, transformation)	**Vanity** (pride, admiration, followers)
Value-added experiences (expansion, variety, adventure)	**Social credit** (open doors, influence others, upward mobility)
Private legacy (accumulation, acquisition, planet and people concerns)	**Public legacy** (ego, perpetuity, service to humanity)

Avanti's discretionary income—her spending power, if you like—will decide whether she steps out to a nearby restaurant for lunch during the week, or whether she gets one of Mumbai's impeccable dabbawalas to deliver a meal to her office. In other words, money will moderate the fulfilment of her motivations. It will determine whether she goes out every night or only on weekends; as indeed it will play a role in many other areas, such as which apartment she rents, how many Uber rides she books and so on.

Avanti's values will guide her choices in many ways. Will she climb the corporate ladder the old-fashioned way, through intelligence, hard work and earning every promotion on merit? Or will she be someone who uses a tradecraft bordering on the edgy to get ahead? Will Avanti use dates to find a long-term partner or will she be strictly short-term? Her values will play a large part in both decisions, as in other similar ones.

Her personality will play a significant role in all this. For example, is her primary instinct 'fight' or 'flight'? Is she fond of company and inclined to go out rather than stay in? Does she enjoy knowing lots of people or just a few? Where does she land on the Myers-Briggs personality type model?

The final influencer is time. Some decisions are for the here and now; others are longer-term. One factor here is the stage of life Avanti is at. She might choose to date in her early twenties to play the field, enjoying a range of companions without being interested in finding 'the one true one'. But it is equally possible that the same Avanti, if still single in her early thirties, might look at dating as a way to find someone to settle into a long-term relationship with.

That's my customer motivation model. I hope it has given you a framework for thinking about customers in present-day India. We will look at some ways to use the model in the next chapter.

III

How Do We Influence People?

Nugget 3: Uses of the Customer Motivation Model

'Ideas are useless unless used. The proof of their value is in their implementation.'

—Theodore Levitt, economist and author of
Marketing for Business Growth

In the previous chapter, I introduced you to my customer motivation model. It can be used in many ways. In this chapter, I present three ways in which the model can be used:

1. For seamless integration of business goals and marketing strategy
2. For value-added customer segmentation
3. For product and brand development

1) Seamless integration of business goals and marketing strategy

Peter Drucker (1909–2005) was a writer, consultant, entrepreneur and journalist memorialized by the *Bloomberg Businessweek* magazine as 'the man who invented management'.[1] He needs little introduction to those in business and marketing. Born in Germany, he emigrated to the United States, where he served as a professor at the Sarah Lawrence College in New York, from 1939 to 1949, and simultaneously worked as a writer. He got his first job as a consultant in 1940, and he also taught at Bennington College in Vermont. Thanks to his popularity, he later received a position to teach in the Graduate School of Business Administration at the New York University.

He was an active contributor for a long period of time to magazines such as the *Atlantic* and was a columnist for the *Wall Street Journal.* The quality and popularity of his writings assured him important contracts both as a writer and as a consultant with large companies, government agencies and non-profit organizations in the United States, Europe, Latin America and Asia.

Drucker is considered one of the most successful exponents of management, to which he devoted sixty years of his life. His ideas and terminologies have influenced the corporate world since the '40s.

---

[1] 'The Man Who Invented Management', *Bloomberg Businessweek*, 28 November 2005, https://www.bloomberg.com/news/articles/2005-11-27/the-man-who-invented-management

His work as a consultant began with General Motors, an association that resulted in his landmark book *Concept of the Corporation* (1946). This was followed by many more books on the theory of management, which are consulted often and regarded as fundamental texts in the field of business management. In 1954, he published *The Practice of Management*, widely considered the first book to organize the art and science of running an organization into an integrated body of information.[2]

While Professor Drucker remains popular at B-schools, his diminished prominence in present-day marketing conversations has less to do with the power of his ideas than with our attraction to shiny new things. To those who, like me, greatly value the incisiveness of his thinking, Professor Drucker has much to offer, no matter the date on the calendar. Many of his ideas remain as relevant to business and marketing today as they were when first presented, despite the many changes in the technology we use and our ways of life.

Pre-eminent among the several brilliant contributions Professor Drucker made is his definition of business purpose: 'The purpose of business is to create and keep a customer.' When I first heard this definition (decades ago, as a student of marketing), it became an immediate and lifelong mantra. The simple sentence works like a sextant, a navigation tool for brand ships sailing the choppy seas of business. It also

---

2   Source: https://www.drucker.institute/perspective/about-peter-drucker/ and
    https://history-biography.com/peter-drucker/

helps bring those who might have drifted off course back to their intended routes.

The purpose of marketing *is to create and keep a customer*

Viewing Professor Drucker's definition of business purpose through a marketing lens, what is immediately apparent is that it sets the agenda for marketing.

Simply and irrevocably:

1) *There is no business without customers*
2) *There is no customer without marketing*
3) *Great marketing is about great brands*
4) *Great brands make and keep more customers*

Business, Customers, Brand. Elementary, I know. But you'd marvel if I told you how many business owners I meet who are facing problems that can be tracked back to them, or their teams, having lost sight of these first principles.

What's specially energizing about this perspective, especially for a marketer, is that it puts marketing at the heart of business. While this might be as clear as crystal to most, it is not uncommon to hear, even today, of businesses that put marketing at the end of the process, as a sort of final gift wrap before delivery.

It is also not uncommon, in this age of prolific tech start-ups, to see engineer-owners and their teams put 99 per cent of their time and budget into product development, processes and people, leaving marketing to the very end of the journey, with next to nothing left in the tank. Sometimes they come out okay, especially when an investor hands the start-up funding for customer acquisition. But such cases are few and far between, and dozens if not hundreds of Indian start-ups struggle, even perish, due to the absence, or patchiness, of early-stage marketing integration.

With creating and keeping customers firmly established as its business purpose, any product or service, including online products and services, must convincingly answer these four questions at the very outset:

1) *Which existing customer problem do we solve?*
2) *Which new ways of life do we make possible?*
3) *Which new benefits, experiences or capabilities do we create?*
4) *How are we better than alternatives to access those benefits, experiences or capabilities?*

No matter how basic it sounds, the inescapable fact is that any product or service has to solve a problem or make a new way of life possible in order to win customers.

Answering questions 1 and 2 precisely gives clarity and focus to the business. Answering them too broadly, or in a self-serving manner, could hamper success. Great answers to those questions create a strong relevance for a product or service. Weak answers to those questions might create fuzzy relevance and poor customer responses.

Questions 3 and 4 are about differentiation; about how new benefits, or new and nuanced versions of existing benefits, can make a product or service more attractive.

Let's look at those four questions bringing my customer motivation model into play.

Imagine we are a business team tasked to launch a new flavoured, carbonated drink, targeting twenty-somethings. It sounds counter-intuitive, I know, because worldwide the market for sweetened, carbonated, flavoured drinks such as Coca-Cola, Pepsi, Sprite, Fanta and Mountain Dew is declining as customers move to other refreshment choices. India is no exception. The market for bottled water—Aquafina, Kinley, Bisleri and a host of other brands—is growing, although plain water's palate profile is quite bland compared to fizzy drinks. (In India, where bottled water combats the perils of unsafe drinking water, it is often a necessity rather than only a vote against flavoured carbonated drinks.) Mineral-, vitamin- and flavour-enriched bottled water is a fledgling trend in India. Club soda has a role as a mixer but is rarely drunk on its own. Red Bull is a draw for youngsters, despite lingering questions about its long-term impact on health due to high levels of sugar and caffeine and the presence of taurine in it. Beer and alcopops, though technically not soft drinks, are making inroads, even with those not legally permitted to drink them, such as teens. Fruit juices are good for health and find some appeal among pre-teens, but are less attractive in social situations. Carbonated fruit juices have repeatedly failed to make a mark in the beverages segment. Premixed, packaged Indian-flavour drinks—like aam panna and jal jeera—are a tiny fraction of the market. Post-exercise hydration drinks—such as Gatorade—is a growing segment but not easy to afford. In a nutshell, there is a considerable churn in the soft-drinks market, with the days of single-format dominance by a cola, lemon or orange brand a wistful memory.

And yet, here we are (in our hypothetical example), looking to launch a new soft drink, bucking the trends, zigging when the world is zagging. Are we condemned to failure even before we are out of the blocks? Not necessarily. What we need is the right place to start. And the place to start is at the *motivators* level, before we plunge into category benefits.

So let's start there. Let's first look at the motivators other products in the segment are using. Bottled waters fulfil a *self-love* need—they help you take better care of yourself while making you feel better about yourself. They are also a *good sense* purchase. Fruit juices and post-exercise hydration drinks broadly share the same two motivators as water. Beers could be about the *joy of ownership*; alcopops about *social credit* (especially among younger customers), as is Red Bull. Colas are purely *hedonistic*—there's little reason to consume one other than pleasure.

In the '60s, '70s and '80s, flavoured fizzy drinks positioned their drinkers as people who lived life fully (*value-added experiences*) and were fun to be with (*connection*). Today, the drinkers of those brands (even low-calorie, low-sugar versions) are seen as less responsible in their choices, less committed to health and fitness, somehow less worthy. There is a sense of unvoiced reproach and guilt attached to the consumption of fizzy drinks. As the team launching the hypothetical new carbonated drink, we must find motivators that not only set free the urge for consumption but also mitigate this guilt and prevent stigma for the consumer. If we accept this as a starting point, which of the several untapped motivators could help us do that? A soft drink can certainly be about *hedonism*. Can it also be about getting *attention*? Can it be about *one-upmanship*, or *vanity*?

Let's say that after analysis, ideation and discussion, the motivators we choose are *hedonism*, *self-love* and *private legacy*. Now that we have chosen them, how does that influence the answers to the four questions posed earlier? Here's what the answers might look like:

1) *Which existing customer problem do you solve?*
   We free twenty-somethings of the guilt attached to the consumption of carbonated flavoured drinks.

2) *Which new ways of life do you make possible?*
   We make it possible for twenty-somethings to enjoy flavoured carbonated drinks as much as they like, as often as they like, wherever they like (*hedonism*) while feeling good about what they put into their bodies (*self-love*) and with responsibility towards the planet (*private legacy*).

3) *Which new experiences or capabilities do you create?*
   The unabashed indulgence of pleasure but not at the cost of good health or at the risk of social censure.

4) *How are you better than other methods of accessing those benefits?*
   We make carbonated drinks from exotic fruits, herbs and berries like Japanese ume plums, Brazilian guarana,

Korean ginseng and Indian amalaki among others. In beer-shaped recyclable bottles and other recyclable social consumption formats. We have our own recycling system, including bins and collection agents.

So there you have it: an example of how the four questions might be answered, using the customer motivation model as the starting point. You might wonder: Why those particular choices, why those particular answers? Those are great questions to ask, although there is no single correct answer. An essential part of strategy is making choices. Every marketing team could choose different motivators, answer the questions differently and come up with a very different business and product idea. Isn't that wonderful? More importantly, this is a hypothetical example meant to illustrate how approaching a business or marketing challenge with motivators as the starting point gets you off the ground in a very different way from other starting points. Finally, accepting this particular set of answers, perhaps it is clear how we have taken a big first step to 'creating and keeping a customer'?

2) Value-added customer segmentation

You cannot be all things to all people. In trying to do so, it is very likely that you will end up satisfying few and displeasing many. In marketing terms, it is much better to mean everything to someone than something to everyone.

In other words, Segmentation. A customer segment is, as we well know, a more or less homogeneous consumption audience you are targeting with your product or brand.

There are several kinds of customer segmentation models. The most widely prevalent ones in use in India today are still, surprisingly, demographic models. Many businesses still define audiences by age, income, urban/rural, metros vs tier-1, -2 or -3 towns, socio-economic class, ownership of appliances and gadgets and so on. These definitions are occasionally overlaid with a sprinkle of attitudes, buying behaviour and media habits. Demographic segmentation models are the legacy of a newspaper and TV media era, when media penetration and consumption were measured in demographic terms, leading to demographics becoming the default segmentation model. While demographics are still useful, they largely serve the interests of mass media sellers and buyers. They don't help as much in designing products and services.

This is not to suggest that marketers are handcuffed to a legacy demographic model. Without doubt, marketers can and do add value to demographic models. In my work, I segment present-day India into two groups—'India Arrived' and 'India Rising'—based on where they stand on the development continuum. India Arrived includes several generations of people with higher education qualifications; they are largely urban, mostly live in apartments, have office jobs which demand more of the mind than of the body, are proficient in English and are tech-savvy users of multiple devices. India Rising has mostly first- or second-generation learners, in lower-end corporate roles or small-sized self-employment, with one foot in rural or agrarian India; they are usually conversant in more than one Indian language, tend to be in trades and professions that require a physical skill set and use technology primarily on mobile phones, though to a relatively limited extent. If the current middle class of around 300 million is India Arrived, there are several hundreds of millions others in India Rising. India Rising wants a life similar to what India Arrived has had for generations. The former are avid purchasers of goods and services that will help their children, if not themselves, to level with India Arrived.

The India Arrived–India Rising model has its uses in understanding the life changes each customer segment is looking for. However, similar to other demographic models, this model too has somewhat limited utility in product and brand design.

With the abundance of customer data available today, there has never been a better time to move towards more nuanced models that better guide product and brand design. A motivators-based model, as illustrated through the hypothetical soft drink example earlier in this chapter, is one such. When we approach customers who choose something from one set of motivators, such as the intersection of *hedonism*, *self-love* and *private legacy* (relating to the planet and other people) in the soft drink example, we *exclude* customers who do not privilege these motivators. We do this with open eyes and a clear sense of choice. Some segments that we exclude comprise those who choose on the basis of *self-love* and *good sense* (bottled water) and those who choose on the basis of *personal reinvention* and *good sense* (post-workout hydrators). The advantage of the motivators-based model is that it does not look at segments by age, geography and income. The segments are homogeneous, based on the personal needs that drive the search for a product or service. Looked at through the lens of motivators, our vast country, indeed the entire world, is flat.

3) Product and brand development

Motivators play a significant role in product and brand design. Let's now look at product design. (The brand design aspect will be covered in the next section of this book, 'How to Craft Your Brand'.)

Certain categories of products are natural fits with certain motivators. Take a look at the chart below.

Customer Motivation Model: Categories

INNER-DIRECTED MOTIVATORS	OUTER-DIRECTED MOTIVATORS
Good sense (toothpaste, private security, online banking)	**One-upmanship** (whisky snobbery, lavish weddings, mobile phones)
Self-love (career, personal interests, yoga)	**FOMO** (groups, travel, entertainment)
Hedonism (food, drink, entertainment, fashion)	**Attention** (clothes, cosmetics, social media)
Joy of ownership (personal vehicles, real estate, jewellery)	**Connection** (dating sites, festival gifting, coffee shops)
Personal reinvention (continuing education, diet advice, life coaches)	**Vanity** (beauty products, hair colour/regrowth, body reshaping)
Value-added experiences (travel, restaurants, interest group affiliations)	**Social credit** (club memberships, wine, owning art)
Private legacy (children's education, books, performing arts)	**Public legacy** (charity, elected office, corporations)

Alongside each motivator are some product categories that align with it strongly. Private security has a lot to do with *good sense*, as does online banking. We can easily relate whisky snobbery and lavish, over-the-top weddings to *one-upmanship*.

A parent keen to leave a *private legacy* might educate his children at certain institutions of repute, no matter the cost. Another might become a writer or leave an immense library to her heirs. Club memberships, knowing how to choose and enjoy wine, and owning art might give one *social credit*. While there is a good fit between motivators and categories, as the model demonstrates, this does not imply a unique association between a particular product category and a particular motivator. Products satisfy multiple motivators. Conversely, motivations are fulfilled by multiple products.

How does my customer motivation model help with product development? Every category has its own features and benefits. Some of these are vital to creating a fundamental relevance for a category, while other features and benefits act as differentiators. The Cadbury brand in India offers a great example of how motivators can help build a dominant share of the market. The flagship Cadbury Dairy Milk's rich, creamy, chocolate taste is a primary feature that earns Cadbury its relevance and preference with customers. It constitutes the table stakes and also a standard—putting Cadbury firmly into the chocolate category and making it the player to beat for any new entrant. But is the taste of Cadbury Dairy Milk a sufficient selling point? Taste responds to the *hedonism* motivator. Cadbury Dairy Milk's creamy taste, supported by the claim that every bar has a glass and a half of milk, wins appeal among children while also helping their mothers step over the 'is chocolate good for my child?' barrier. The Cadbury product range proves that there are plenty of opportunities to differentiate even within the primary motivator of *hedonism*—through Dairy

Milk variants such as roast almond and caramel, and through value-added ranges such as Silk, Temptations and Bournville, which touch the *value-added experiences* motivator. Then there are Cadbury products that interact with the *good sense* motivator, such as Bournvita malted chocolate drink. Five Star was originally positioned, back in the '70s, as a chocolate bar you shared with someone else, making use of the *connection* motivator. In addition to these, the Cadbury Celebrations gift packs provide *social credit* during festivals and special occasions. My point is that in every category, one or more motivators must be touched in order to create primary relevance for the product (*hedonism* in Cadbury's case), but still, the entire map of fourteen motivators (and sub-motivators), with all its multiple features and benefits, is available for further exploration (Cadbury makes use of *good sense, connection* and *social credit*). It also opens up adjacent customer segments, such as, in the Cadbury example, adults, teens, seniors and gifting.

In the first three chapters of this book, we've looked at a new way to understand people as customers. My new customer motivation model helps marketers do that. With this foundation in place, we will look at the art of crafting brands in the next section.

Section 2

How to Craft Your Brand

IV

Where Do Brands Come From?

*Nugget 4: Learning from the Past
to Shape Tomorrow's Brands*

'*It takes many good deeds to build a good reputation, and
only one bad one to lose it.*'

—Benjamin Franklin

In the first chapter of this book, 'Who Are We Talking
To?', we looked at the evolution of the multiple-identity
customer; in the second, 'Why Do People Buy?', I
introduced you to my customer motivation model; and
in the third, 'How Do We Influence People?', we looked
at ways in which needs and motivators can drive product
design and relevance.

Brands are differentiated agglomerations of features
and benefits, with unique identities and personalities
which provide gratifications to customers based on their
motivations. Brands have been with humankind, in some

shape or form, for pretty much all of recorded history. In Section 2, we'll look at crafting a brand. We'll do that mostly in Chapters 5 and 6. But before that, in this chapter, we'll look at the evolution of brands and its implications on present-day branding.

1) Early man

Hidden in the jungles of the Maros-Pangkep region on Sulawesi island in Indonesia is a cave called Leang Timpuseng. The cave is not easy to reach. Once inside, the rocks seem to close in on the visitor. Leang Timpuseng is of widespread interest for the cave art on its walls, discovered by Dutch explorers in the 1950s. Preserved here, above head height, are stencils of human hands, albeit now somewhat faint and faded, against a background of red paint. Equally exciting is a just-visible line drawing of an animal, a babirusa or deer-pig, native to that habitat. Maxime Aubert, an archaeologist and geochemist from Griffith University in Queensland, Australia used a technique he developed to date the painting. At least 35,400 years old, it is *the world's first known picture*, supplanting from that position the ancient cave art in Spain and France, long believed to be the oldest on Earth.

The 2014 announcement of these findings was fascinating not just to academics and art historians but also to marketing theorists of a certain bent of mind—such as myself. The babirusa drawing casts fresh light on the human mind and on our capacity for imagination and symbolism. Jo Marchant, the author of an article on the subject in *Smithsonian* magazine, writes, 'Such sophisticated thinking was a huge competitive advantage . . . It also opened the door to imaginary realms and a host of intellectual and emotional connections that infused our lives with meaning beyond the basic impulse to survive. And because it enabled symbolic thinking—our ability to let one thing stand for another—it allowed people to make visual representations of the things they could remember and imagine.'[1]

Why are the Leang Timpuseng cave paintings of interest from a brand history point of view? For a number of reasons, which are collectively persuasive that the paintings are ancient precursors of modern-day brands and marketing. The paintings are the first human depictions of life; much of marketing is, to this date, depictions of human life— sometimes real; at other times exaggerated into caricatures or idylls. The paintings reveal our attraction for symbols, our ability to imagine and interpret, our emotional connections to objects and living things, our need to bring meaning into our lives, taking them beyond questions of mere survival. These human needs and ideas are very much central in branding and marketing. When we try to imagine the unknown Leang Timpuseng painter, we see someone who went beyond the basic hunter-gatherer or homemaker-child-rearer to display remarkable and differentiated gifts. The ability to recreate the things the tribe witnessed every day must have set the painter apart as 'the one who can draw', someone with a higher-order skill set which undoubtedly must have secured a higher stature. Depictions of life, identifiable

[1]   Jo Marchant, 'A Journey to the Oldest Cave Paintings in the World', *Smithsonian*, January 2016, https://www.smithsonianmag.com/history/journey-oldest-cave-paintings-world-180957685/

symbols, differentiation, competitive advantage, stature—all ingredients of modern-day branding and marketing.

Back home and closer in time, the Bhimbetka rock shelters in Madhya Pradesh (forty-five kilometres from Bhopal) are a UNESCO World Heritage Site. They give fascinating evidence of advancements in ancient man's depictions of life—in terms of not just the quality of paintings but also the complexity of ideas, subjects and images portrayed. The first archaeological team to visit Bhimbetka was led by V.S. Wakankar in 1957, but the scale and significance of the rock shelters came to national attention in the 1970s, with the discovery of artefacts, wares and the now-famous rock paintings.

The paintings, deep in the inner recesses, are made from vegetable dyes and have lasted centuries. The oldest Bhimbetka paintings are 10,000 years old, a time-jump of 25,000 years from Leang Timpuseng. What is unique about Bhimbetka is that its paintings provide a continuous record of human advancement, similar to annual report cards, except they cover centuries instead of years. The rock shelters saw unbroken occupation by successive generations for several hundred years, and each generation left their paintings on the walls. These provide us with a timeline of the people who made the Bhimbetka paintings, which experts classify into seven different periods. Period 1 has linear representations, in green and dark red, of huge figures of bison, tigers and rhinoceroses. Period 2 has smaller stylized figures in which, in addition to animals, we see human figures in hunting scenes, armed with spears, bows and arrows. There are also images of tribal wars, with tribes symbolized and differentiated by their individual animal totems. There are images of communal dances, musical instruments, pregnant women, children, drinking scenes and burials. Period 3 paintings portray the cave-dwellers in contact with neighbouring agricultural communities and exchanging goods with them. Periods 4 and 5, now incorporating a change in colours to red, white and yellow, depict riders, tunic-like dresses and religious symbols such as nature spirits (*yakshas*), tree gods and magical sky chariots. Finally, periods 6 and 7 have more schematic, geometric, linear images, albeit in a cruder art style. One rock depicts elephants, swamp deer and bison. Others show a peacock, snake, deer and the sun, tusked elephants, wild boars, horsemen and archers. And in what could be one of the most recent of these paintings, in one of the desolate rock shelters, we see a man holding a trident-like staff as he dances. This painting was given the name *Nataraja* by Wakankar.[2]

The Bhimbetka paintings not only tell a wonderful story of the ever-increasing complexity in the cave-dwellers' lives, there is also much to interest the brand and marketing enthusiast. We see animal totem symbols to differentiate tribes (early logos?); we see competition for resources in the wars they fought against each other; we see beneficial alliances with neighbours, who had complementary goods like agricultural produce for trade. Equally, we see differentiation in skill sets: hunters armed with increasingly complex weaponry and methods; planters and growers of grain and other produce; and many more painters,

---

increasingly diverse in style. We see depictions of early religion, signalling the emergence of a new sophistication in the thought and societies of that time. All these are forerunners of the ideas and practices that resonate loudly in present-day marketing.

From this seemingly modest beginning, it is not difficult to project how branding as we know it today must have come into being. As ancient societies evolved, new skill sets emerged to meet new lifestyle requirements. Pottery, clothing, tools of trade and a host of products became available. Multiple providers of each would have meant a range of qualities and prices; it would have generated the need to identify the maker of a preferred item and where to find that person. This would have given birth to unique symbols stamped on each jar or tunic or axe, identifying the maker and location, so that customers would visit him or her and commerce could be conducted. The brand, as we know it today, was off and running.

2) Knights Templar

The Poor Fellow-Soldiers of Christ and of the Temple of Solomon, which is the full name of the Catholic monastic-military order widely known as the Knights Templar, were at their peak a group of approximately 20,000 members, of which about 10 per cent were knights. The 90 per cent non-combatant members were either highly skilled in finance (even inventing a novel method of banking) or supported the Knights in battle. Founded in the twelfth century, initially to protect pilgrims preyed on by highwaymen on their way to the Holy Land, the Knights grew rapidly in membership and power and soon were, resplendent in their white mantles bearing a red cross, among the most skilled fighting units in the Crusades. The flag they carried into battle also bore a large red cross set against two solid horizontal halves, the upper black and the lower white. Symbolizing their vow of individual poverty (the knights held no property, had no wealth and earned no riches), their emblem or seal depicted two riders on a single horse. In their later years, however, the order became wealthy, not just through innovative banking but also by reaching across borders to form what some suggest was the world's first multinational corporation. This must undoubtedly have been aided by a papal order that permitted the Templars to pass through borders without being stopped or paying taxes, as they were answerable only to the Pope.

The Templars' reputation also grew owing to their military tactics and successes. They were famous for never retreating from battle unless outnumbered three to one, and only if commanded. If no command was received, they would fight to the death. Templars would often lead key battles. Heavily armoured knights on heavily armoured horses would use the 'squadron charge', wherein a tightly formed unit of horsemen would act as a battering ram, without fear of their lives, to blast a hole through enemy lines. These methods gave them famous victories, among them the Battle of Montgisard in 1177, in which 500 Templar Knights helped an infantry unit of a few thousands beat Saladin's army of over 26,000.

The Templars' decline came through a combination of factors, not least among which were the concerns voiced by their two most powerful rival orders, the Knights Hospitaller and the Teutonic Knights. European nobles, nervous about the Templars' financial might and independence, added their weight to the opposition. But the weightiest of voices against them was that of France's King Philip IV, who mistrusted the Templars as they had declared a desire to form their own state in an area in south-eastern France, with the island of Cyprus as an option. These factors—plus the fact that Philip IV had inherited an impoverished kingdom from his father and was already deeply in debt to the Templars—were probably what led to his actions: in 1307 Philip IV ordered the arrest of many Templars for blasphemy, had them confess under duress to crimes against Christianity and put them to death. The popular opinion was that Philip was jealous of the Templars and had brought false charges against them to renege on his debt and seize their financial resources for himself. Finally, in 1312, Philip IV put Pope Clement V under extreme pressure, leading to an edict dissolving the order.[3]

The Knights Templar are interesting from a brand and marketing point of view on many levels. Chief among these is their unshakeable belief in their way of life. Great brands have beliefs about themselves and the world they occupy and create, as Facebook and Evian demonstrate. The Templars had unique visual identifiers in their white mantles and red cross. Great brands have long-standing and well-regarded identifiers, such as Coke's iconic bottle, Shell's oyster shell and the golden arches of McDonald's. The Templars' battle

---

[3]   Source: https://www.ancient.eu/Knights_Templar/ and https://www.history.com/topics/middle-ages/the-knights-templar

strategies and tactics were theirs and theirs alone. Great brands have remarkable go-to-market plans, as Apple and Netflix are known for. The Templars had unique financial practices and the cross-border reach of a multinational. Amazon is a great modern-day example of clever financial practices and cross-border reach. Finally, the Templars were done for, thanks to the actions of their competitors. Weren't Kodak, Nokia and Blackberry, and aren't most brands? Yet, standing tall years after their decline and fall is the Templars' brand legend. The kind of legend most brands aspire to create for themselves.

3) American cattlemen

The American cowboy astride his horse—with wide-brimmed hat, colourful bandana, checked shirt, buckskin vest, leather chaps, holstered six-gun, sheathed rifle and tinkling spurs—is an iconic figure of nineteenth-century America. He was glorified in books by writers such as Louis L'Amour and Zane Grey, and in films, in which he was played by larger-than-life actors such as John Wayne and later, in a darker avatar, by Clint Eastwood. The cowboy was young, guileless, hard-working, honest, respectful of women and loyal to the outfit he rode for. The outfit was a ranch with a house, corrals and other buildings; the boss was the rancher; the work was raising cattle for beef, to feed the ever-growing and ever-hungry towns.

While the rancher, his cowboys and herds of cattle on a drive are abiding images of America's great push westwards, the origin of ranching—which involves raising large herds of animals and managing them from horseback—as well as the origin of the cowboy tradition, can be traced to Spain. Members of the Spanish nobility received large land grants that the Kingdom of Castile had captured from the Moors. They were to defend that land and could use it to earn money. They pioneered open-range breeding of sheep and cattle as the most efficient method of utilizing vast swathes of land to generate revenue for themselves.

When the conquistadors came to America in the sixteenth century, followed by the settlers, Spanish cattle management and raising techniques came with them. Large land grants from the Spanish and later Mexican governments allowed large numbers of animals to roam free over what is now northern Mexico and southern Texas. The vaquero tradition of north Mexico grew from the interaction between the Spanish elites and the native and mestizo peoples. As settlers in the United States moved west, they brought cattle raised on the east coast and in Europe with them but borrowed many elements of the vaquero culture and cattle traditions. So was born the American cowboy, who would take such a strong hold of the popular imagination and culture in times to come.

As the number of ranches increased, the open range came under pressure not just by herds of cattle and horses but also by farmers who were required to raise the grain to feed a growing population and their livestock. In time, the battle for range became very competitive, as did the need for a rancher to claim as his own every single legitimate animal on his land. And this created the need for an indelible, unique, visible mark to be put on cattle and horses, to show that they belonged to particular individuals. That mark was 'the brand'.

The word brand is believed to have been derived from the Old Norse word *brandr*, meaning to burn. This seems to have a connection with real life since the mark a rancher put on his cattle was burnt into the animals' hides using a fire-heated branding iron.

Needless to say, not every cowboy and not every rancher was honest. Rustling—or stealing someone else's cattle—was common, despite it being a criminal offence and facing a high risk of street justice, including being shot or hanged by those who caught you in the act. In the days prior to branding, it must have been well-nigh impossible to prove a cow belonged to you, since all cattle of a certain strain were identical. Branding put an end to casual rustling but did not prevent intrepid rustlers from altering brands by burning their own brand over the original brand—their own brand designed, of course, so that it would easily cover and modify the original.

From a marketing perspective, the brands of the American West display many of the practices of modern-day branding. First, the need to differentiate that which is yours from all other similar products, or in other words, to raise your product above the sameness of commodities. Second, the use of an indelible, unique, identifying mark that signals ownership. A trademark, if you like. Third, assuming a rancher had good stock, fed on good grass and raised with good practices that increased their meat yield, it is easy to see how a brand would be attributed with features and benefits, thereby raising its value in the market. Fourth, the robust protection of the brand, the trademark, from rustlers and thieves, who might attempt to overlay it with their own. Fifth, the acquisition of goodwill: if a rancher was a man of his word, with his brand maintaining its standards drive after drive, such that cattle buyers would come to rely on his quality and delivery, he would earn trust, reputation and preferred status from customers.

4) The twentieth-century brand

The twentieth century is significant in many ways. Prosperity grew in the advanced countries, while less advantaged countries began their climb out of poverty. More people across the world were able to afford more things. This led to the rise of consumption, and the desire to own and use better products and brands. Many new corporations came into being. They began to manufacture a range of products that made improvements to the quality of life, no matter where on the planet one lived. Needless to say, competition for customers grew.

These changes led to the flourishing of marketing, branding and advertising. By the '60s and '70s, as portrayed in the popular American TV show *Mad Men*, advertising had become so central to the marketing of brands that the doyens of the profession were superstars. This centrality created an entire industry, an industry that was influential, creative and irreplaceable for the success of businesses. From a marketing perspective, the twentieth century was the Century of Advertising.

It is interesting to look at some of the brands that started with the century, many of which are still among us today.

In 1900 Rudolf Diesel demonstrated his diesel engine, running it on peanut oil (the first biofuel?). In the same year, Wilhelm Maybach designed an engine which was built at Daimler-Motoren-Gesellschaft, following the specifications of Emil Jellinek, who asked for the engine to be named Daimler-Mercedes after his daughter Mercedes. In 1902, the Mercedes 35 hp, with the Maybach engine, went into production at Daimler. The year 1900 also saw the launch of the Brownie camera, which later led to the formation of Eastman Kodak. Ford Model A was launched in 1903, followed by the Model T in 1908. Jonteel Talc for women appeared in 1900. Pond's Extract, first launched in 1846, was by the early 1900s popular as a medicinal product that worked on blisters, sprains and skin conditions and also as a 'family doctor for colds and inflammation'. William Colgate's small soap and candles company, started in 1806 and reorganized to be managed by his son as the Colgate Company after his death in 1857, initially launched a number of perfumed soaps. In 1896, Colgate launched toothpaste in a collapsible tube, the product line that it is most recognized for today. If you were a smoker in the 1900s, Sweet Caporal cigarettes wanted you to consider them.

As the century advanced, the Chevrolet Roadster came into being, as did Ivory soap, Lux laundry flakes, Pond's vanishing cream (which, fascinatingly, used advertising in 1923 to draw women's attention to the 'lines on the face as signs of ageing', a problem statement that many a face-care brand uses to this day), Pepsodent (for white teeth) and Lifebuoy (then mild and pure for shampooing 'bobs', the preferred hairstyle among fashionable women of that time).

By the '60s and '70s, a range of powerful brand images had been created. The Marlboro Man, born in 1962, still commands our imagination, even though cigarettes themselves have been revealed as harmful to personal and public health. Virginia Slims ('You've come a long way, baby'), BMW ('The ultimate driving machine'), Ronald McDonald, the Energizer Bunny, Tide, Kodak, Persil . . . a whole range of brands, and their advertising campaigns, had made our homes their own.

The '70s saw an explosion of consumer electronics, with video players, TVs, music systems and portable cassette players from Sony, Hitachi, Toshiba and a host of Japanese brands wanting a share of our entertainment wallets. The late '80s and '90s saw the dawn of the personal computer, and Compaq, IBM, Apple and Lotus were soon common household names. This also marked the arrival of early models of the mobile phone, with Nokia, Ericsson and Motorola among the leading players. The 1964-born Nike was taking giant strides towards becoming the fitness industry colossus it now is. Heritage clothing brands like Levi Strauss & Co., founded in 1853, climbed new heights while also starting to move denim away from its legacy positioning of blue-collar utility towards hip urban fashion. New brands like Gap, founded in 1969, tapped into casual everyday dressing, even as the world's fashion giants like Gucci, Prada and Armani expanded their product footprints to strengthen their hold on the luxury market.

As we entered the last decade of the '90s and started to look ahead to the 2000s, the imminent convergence between telephony, the Internet, video, email and shopping had become clear. Blackberry was an early mover and soon built a strong reputation as the best email-friendly handheld device. New products and brands were soon to appear, like the iPhone from Apple, as well as Facebook, Instagram and WhatsApp. These would profoundly change the way we live, as the first two decades of the twenty-first century have demonstrated.

India has its own history of brands through the 1900s. Unlike the West, which saw a rapid brand diversification in a range of categories, pre-Independence Indian brands were largely in the construction, utilities, manufacturing, banking and textile sectors, especially for the first three decades or so of the century. Allahabad Bank (which was founded in 1865), Godrej & Boyce, Indian Hotels Company Limited, Calcutta Electric Supply Corporation, Shalimar Paints, Phoenix Mills, Bank of India, Tata Steel, Bank of Baroda, Tata Power, Kesoram Cotton Mills, Kansai Nerolac Paints and Glaxo Laboratories are eminent among them. Alongside this 'industrial' core, brands like Nestlé, Britannia, Bata, Raymond, Imperial Tobacco, Vazir Sultan Tobacco, Hindustan Vanaspati (the Indian subsidiary of Lever Brothers, which later merged into Lever Brothers India), Godfrey Phillips, Eveready, TVS and Air India offered personal consumption items. Most of the pre-1947 companies had British or Parsi, Gujarati and Marwari promoters. By the second half of the twentieth century, post-independence India stepped away from its colonial past and diversified into a wide range of companies and brands. The period saw the launch of Binaca, an iconic toothpaste brand from the '50s through to the '70s, alongside Geoffrey Manners' Forhan's and Colgate. It saw Murphy

Radio, Lifebuoy, Wills Navy Cut and Amul Butter. It saw the transformation of the steel trading company Mahindra & Mohammed, which became Mahindra & Mahindra, initially the assemblers of Willys jeeps in India and soon crowned as one of the country's leading automakers. Dalda helped Indian housewives cook treats for their families. When George Fernandes, India's maverick industry minister in the late '70s, created the conditions that led to IBM and Coca-Cola leaving India in 1977, it opened up space for Indian tech companies like HCL and Wipro to enter. Parle Products, already famous for Parle-G, launched Thums Up, Gold Spot and Limca to fill the vacuum left by Coke, Fanta and Sprite with great success. In the '80s, tiny Nirma so badly alarmed Hindustan Unilever's Surf that the multinational giant invented an entirely new business model to launch a new brand called Wheel, which then successfully competed for a share of the rapidly growing washing powder market. Vazir Sultan added Charms to Charminar, even as Bajaj (with its Chetak), Hero Motorcycles, Reliance (Vimal), various arms of the Birla family and a host of other companies launched a wide array of brands to create India's present energetic and thriving consumption landscape. As we entered the 2000s, home-grown brands in the tech space showed promise but disappointingly, they flared only briefly before fading—as Micromax did—or selling to a Western giant, as was the case with Flipkart.

Any mention of marketing in the '90s would not be complete without mention of the advertising men and women who shaped the images and campaigns that built the brands we know so well. International greats like Leo

Burnett, Bill Bernbach, David Ogilvy, Raymond Rubicam, Rosser Reeves and the Saatchi brothers invented a profession and brought both art and science to it. They built their towering reputations on brave and breakthrough campaigns that are remembered with fondness and reverence to this day. The agencies they built gave the advertising industry form and substance as well as all its future leaders. In their time, advertising was about 'creativity that sells', and the names on the door approached it as a day job. In India, figures like Subroto Sengupta, Tara Sinha, Kersy Katrak and Alyque Padamsee stand tall in the profession; they are India's equivalents to the advertising stars of the West.

In the last two decades of the twentieth century, advertising went from being a 'charismatic, individual-led, craft-first, money-second' discipline to becoming a 'global, corporation-led, money-first, craft-second' pursuit. Finance men like the former WPP head Martin Sorrell wrested control of advertising agencies, attracted by their strong customer relationships and high margins. Agency ownership was the platform on which they built global empires and acquired personal wealth. But as this happened, the profession lost more than these new owners gained. It was like one-sided love, in which someone so badly wants the affection and admiration unreciprocated by another that they crush the life out of the very person they love. The spate of takeovers damaged the very thing that had made agencies great in the first place: creativity, as an art and as a science. If the '50s, '60s and '70s saw a blossoming of the advertising profession, the '80s, '90s and early 2000s witnessed its irreversible decline, all the way down to its present precarious position.

All through the tumultuous twentieth century, brands, in general, continued to grow. Brands that failed to adapt to changing times—famously, Kodak and Nokia—have become fractions of their former sizes. New brands like Facebook and Apple are large and attractive today but are facing new regulatory, innovation and manufacturing challenges. Below the radar of these attention-grabbing stories, the vast majority of brands are adapting or reinventing to continue their journeys.

5) The twenty-first-century brand

Where are we today on the brand continuum? What does a brand need to be as we set out on the third decade of the twenty-first century and look ahead towards an uncertain future?

In Chapter 1 of this book, I shared my conviction that the multi-personality customer is the new normal. Customers look to brands to satisfy multiple concurrent needs. To succeed in this multifaceted examination, brands must present many faces of themselves, while preserving their integrity and authenticity. Simple, one-dimensional ideas that served brands well in the previous century—brand positioning, for example—are insufficient to describe and detail twenty-first-century brands. A new brand model is required. I'll share my model, which I call the Brand Octagon, in the next chapter.

V

How Did Brands Get Here?

Nugget 5: Brand Octagon Model for the Twenty-First Century

'Better to make a good future than predict a bad one.'

—Isaac Asimov

'You create a good future by creating a good present.'

—Eckhart Tolle

In the previous chapter I traced the arrival and evolution of brands over the human timeline, starting from early man to the present, with a few significant pit stops on the way. I ended the chapter observing that a new model to describe and detail multifaceted brands was required. I call my model the Brand Octagon.

To my mind, the Brand Octagon serves the needs of the twenty-first-century brand far more comprehensively than other ideas of representing brands. Let's take a closer look at the Brand Octagon in this chapter. But before we do that, let us revisit the ideas that have served brands well in their journey through time.

Way back at the start of the 1900s, a brand was essentially a set of features and benefits with a name. In other words, brands were *commodities with names*. Brands frequently took their inventors' or promoters' names—Colgate, Larsen & Toubro, Lever Brothers—and offered generic category benefits. As more and more products were conceived and manufactured to meet an ever-increasing range of needs, brands which were essentially 'commodities with names' offering generic benefits multiplied manifold through the first half of the century.

By the '60s and '70s, when multiple brands from multiple brand owners competed to offer the same category benefits, it became necessary to draw each brand apart, by giving it an individual name and identity, which made each brand uniquely attractive to a different set of customers. One way to differentiate brands, particularly when product differences became harder to engineer, was through emotional associations with the name. Brands became *products with names that were 'positioned' with imagery*. Among Indian cigarettes, Wills Navy Cut was sensitive and sophisticated, Four Square was rugged and adventurous, Charminar was strong and earthy, and Charms was for the young and free.

The '80s was the decade of the *brand idea*. This was an evolved and a more sophisticated version of the previous decade's *brand positioning*. The intention behind the brand idea was to provide a brand with a strong competitive posture while creating powerful bonds between customers and the brand. Typically, brand ideas sprang from within the category benefits: something in the product made the brand idea believable. Rin detergent, containing sodium tripolyphosphate and other chemicals which washed clothes whiter than oil-based laundry soaps, used the brand idea 'Whiteness that sets you apart' (presented in advertising through a white vs off-white comparison). Surf detergent, also containing similar chemicals, opted for the 'Quality is better value' idea, personified by the character Lalitaji, who became advertising's iconic smart shopper. In the same category, Nirma went with 'Cheap is not inferior' and showed in its ads affluent women using Nirma, to make the brand more attractive to budget-constrained housewives who made up the bulk of its customers.

By the '90s and into the 2010s, image, idea and emotional differentiation had become hard to come by, what with a plethora of brands elbowing each other for attention. This led brands to search for a higher platform to appeal to customers, one that sat above the (by now commonplace) brand idea. Brands looked to create stature by speaking to customers at a human and social level, not just at a product performance level. This approach came to be referred to as the *brand ideal*. The American brand Dove is an example. Despite being a beauty brand, Dove chose to challenge beauty industry stereotypes with its brand ideal. The typical beauty brand presents itself through perfectly made-up supermodels and extensively retouched images of impossibly beautiful women. In the late '90s, Dove took a diametrically opposite approach. Its ideal of 'real beauty' glorified women as they truly are, in all their many sizes, shapes and skin tones. Dove invited women to celebrate their natural beauty in the face of industry campaigns promoting a manipulated flawlessness.

Another example: premium global laundry detergent brand Omo (Surf in India). In the early 2000s, the category of washing powders was saturated with parity-performance brands. This did not prevent some brands from making exaggerated performance and ingredient claims. As a consequence, customers had stopped listening to, believing in and using laundry advertising to choose between brands. Market shares were static and growth was hard to come by. Omo was the first to break from the category's inertia. The long-held laundry convention was that dirt and stains are disrupters of life, bringing embarrassment and shame to people. To make a good impression and attain social success, dirt and stains were to be avoided at all costs. Omo turned this convention on its head. Instead of avoiding dirt, Omo invited consumers to go out and get dirty, because many of life's most rewarding moments involved getting dirty. Sport, a family picnic, goofing around in a park, investigating the mysteries of nature: leading a normal, active life entails getting dirty. As a detergent powerful enough to clean even the toughest stains, Omo gave people the licence to get dirty, to enjoy the activities that made life rich and fulfilling. Omo's brand ideal 'Dirt is good' ('*Daag acche hain*' in India) is a clever counter-category stance for a laundry detergent.

The third example is the global packaged food brand Knorr, which aimed to reverse the worldwide trend of families eating separately, at different times, in different rooms. Its mid-2000s brand ideal, 'the magic of mealtimes', encouraged families to eat together, drawing attention to the many valuable benefits eating together brought to families. These benefits are well-documented: children in families that eat together have larger vocabularies, are more confident, are interested in a wider range of subjects and are more attuned to current affairs. Families that eat together are better bonded and are more likely to reap the emotional rewards of homes and relationships.

'*Jaago Re*', exhorted Tata Tea, asking India to open its eyes to social ups and downs and be more alert to—and keen to change—the status quo around us. Jaago Re is another example of the brand ideal.

By the early 2010s, the allure of brand ideals had faded in the face of criticism that they pushed brands into spaces beyond those they could legitimately occupy. Knorr, for example, is primarily packaged soups and stock cubes. The critics of the 'magic of mealtimes' brand ideal questioned whether Knorr could take as high a ground on a social cause as it aspired to, given its relatively diminutive role in the preparation of family meals.

Former Procter & Gamble global CMO Jim Stengel is an admirer and advocate of the brand ideal. In his 2011 book *Grow: How Ideals Power Growth and Profit at the World's Greatest Companies*, Stengel makes the case that companies who centre their businesses on improving people's lives dominate categories, and have growth rates triple to that of their competitors, with much higher margins than the market average. Another expression for brand ideal, a recent mutation perhaps, which Stengel uses often in his *The CMO Podcast* (available on Spotify), is *brand purpose*.

Which brings us to the present, a time when the power of customers is higher than ever before, on account of social media. As we start the 2020s, brands have a new calling. Whether senior citizens or Gen Z, customers seek genuineness and authenticity in brands. The customer expectation of *brand authenticity* means brands cannot fake things any more: if customers discover irregularities, falsehoods or deliberate bad practices, they are feral in their attacks on brands. This combination of the desire for authenticity on the part of the customer and the present-day, multifaceted nature of brands makes the Brand Octagon particularly potent in our time.

The Brand Octagon

The Brand Octagon provides a template to create authentic brands, which are not just holistic through and through, but also have a powerful competitive advantage.

A brand's *core*, also called brand essence by some marketers, is best defined in relation to the two or three principal perceptions customers have about a brand. In well-managed brands, customers' perceptions are exactly in line with what the brand intends. For successful brand management, customer perceptions can and should be orchestrated to align with the brand's marketing goals. To achieve this orchestration, brands need to answer three questions well.

Q1. *Why are you here?* Why do you—the brand—exist? What do you believe in? Apple might answer this with, 'We think differently about technology.' (My words, not theirs.) Amazon might answer with, 'We believe shopping should come to the customer, as opposed to the customer going to shop.' (Again, my words, not theirs.)

Q2. *What do you do?* Apple: 'We make using technology a pleasure.' Amazon: 'We bring a megastore into your home.'

Q3. *How do you do it?* Apple: 'Our approach to design and aesthetics results in products that are enjoyable to use.' Amazon: 'We make thousands of brands available to you through online shopping and deliver your purchases to your homes.'

This core led Apple to imagine and manufacture products of unusual quality and ease of use. Not very long ago, Apple fans used to wait in breathless anticipation to see which new product their brand would launch. Customers pre-ordered the new products and waited for hours for delivery outside

Apple Stores on launch day, in unending queues. While some of that excitement has abated in present times, perhaps due to the absence of startling new products, Apple continues to rate very high in terms of product quality and demand.

If the average Apple customer says, 'Apple products are different. They are a pleasure to use. I like how they look and feel,' then Apple's intended brand image and perceived brand image are in perfect alignment. If the average Amazon customer says, 'Amazon brings me any brand I want right to my home. They make shopping easy and fun,' then again, the perceived brand image is the intended brand image. *When a perceived brand image is perfectly aligned to the intended brand image, assuming of course the intended brand image has powerful customer appeal, this is reliably good for business.*

Astute readers will have made the connection between the three questions in this chapter relating to *brand core* and the three questions relating to *customers* in Chapter 3 of this book. As a reminder, here are those three questions from Chapter 3:

1) *Which existing customer problem do we solve?*
2) *Which new ways of life do we make possible?*
3) *Which new experiences or capabilities do we create?*

In a good pair of marketing hands, the two sets of parallel questions, one about consumers' needs and the other about brand intentions, come together in a single set of answers. Great marketers intertwine customer insight seamlessly into a brand's core.

The fourth question about customers in Chapter 3 was this:

4) *How are you better than other modes of accessing those benefits?*

The next eight points, presented next to each of the eight sides of the Brand Octagon, individually and collectively answer this single question. Each of them makes a contribution to the answer, some more than others, depending on customer motivations.

1. Performance

The degree of satisfaction a brand provides to customers in terms of functional, emotional and life benefits is the measure of its performance. The product has a large part to play in creating customer satisfaction. A brand must provide *superior* satisfaction to other available choices to be successful, and this underlines the competitive aspect of performance. Competitiveness comes from differentiation; the differentiation must be noticeable and highlight important benefits. It must bring added value to the fundamental task the customer is using the product for. Differentiation on relatively minor benefits is not worthless but will have less of a preference-shaping impact.

Differentiated performance comes from a profound understanding of the customers' needs and motivations that drive a category's usage. An equally deep understanding of the myriad benefits within a category is also required to separate the primary drivers of consumption and preference from the less influential secondary and tertiary drivers.

In regard to Apple's MacBook Air, for example, a customer's performance criteria—in other words, the principal category drivers—are likely to be computing power and easy-to-use software. If the MacBook Air fails to provide these to the customers' satisfaction, at a level at least equal to if not better than the other laptops in the market, then regardless of its obvious design and aesthetic advantages, the MacBook Air will fail customers on performance. If this were to continue over an extended period, customers will reject the MacBook Air and choose from the alternatives, even if these brands don't have products that equal the MacBook Air in design and aesthetics.

Amazon's performance rests on the range of brands offered on its website, how low the price points are and how fast the speed of delivery is. Amazon is responsible for making these the principal category drivers. If for some reason Amazon ends up only as good as all the other e-commerce players, or worse than them, it stands to lose a share of customer shopping occasions, despite its stellar role in pioneering the Internet shopping category.

2. Product interface

Back in the '70s and '80s, the Indian passenger car market had mainly two brands: Premier Automobiles and Hindustan Motors (HM). Most car owners went with one or the other, although a rare model from the third manufacturer, Standard, did turn up here and there. These cars were

Indian remakes of old models of the Italian Fiat and British Morris Oxford, which were Premier and HM's respective technology collaborators. Import substitution and the need to keep costs low meant that many parts were made in India. Over time, both car brands became almost wholly Indian. The Ambassador (by HM) was large and sturdy, while the Premier was smaller and smarter looking. How primitive these cars were, compared to the cars we now have! The gears often didn't engage and had to be gnashed into place. A few kilometres' drive up an incline would be enough to overheat the cars; a fleet of them pulled over on the side of the highway to cool down was not an uncommon sight. The windows often failed to roll down; and if they did roll down, they failed to roll up again. The indicator lamps were prone to failing; the seats were non-reclining and uncomfortable. If these brands gave Indian passenger-car drivers any satisfaction at all, it was in getting them from one place to another in reasonably good shape and time.

The Maruti 800, made in collaboration with Suzuki Motors, joined India's car market in the early '80s. It was an almost instant success. Although small in size, it was quick to accelerate and easy to drive; its gears engaged faultlessly; the indicator stalk snapped back into place after a turn was completed; the windows went up and down smoothly; and the malicious rumour that the Maruti 800 did not have sufficient pep under the hood to climb slopes was quickly proven false. The success of the Maruti 800 was built on a better user interface: all the drive-quality enhancing features a car needed were available, and every feature was vastly better and easier to use.

Fast forward to today's Indian car market and all the admirable features of the original Maruti 800—and a whole host of subsequent innovations—are standard issue. Indian buyers consider power steering, power windows, ORVM lights and music systems entry-level features. The industry standards have been changed forever by the foreign brands that have come into India since the launch of the Maruti 800. They have permanently raised the bar on what a car's user interface should be like—much to the delight of the Indian motorist.

User interface improvements are seen across pretty much every category. Banking is one such. While visiting a bank branch to interact with a teller is still a common practice among senior citizens and small-town customers, most urban Indians use ATMs for cash and Internet banking for services such as money transfers, fixed deposits and car loan repayments. Automation in banking not only provides users with an easy-to-navigate interface for personal banking, it also reduces costs for the brands.

Coming back to the two brands we've been using to illustrate the Brand Octagon, Apple's and Amazon's respective user interfaces have contributed significantly to their success. Using Apple products is easy and rewarding. Amazon ensures its website performs better than the competition, in both desktop and, importantly for India, mobile versions. Amazon's user interface has many features—filters for sorting brands, comparing options, referring to past searches, suggestions of similar products, user reviews, effortless payment and so on. All these make the interface simple and pleasing—and the brand increasingly desirable.

3. Pricing

What does a brand's price tell you? Price is at once so many things. It declares a brand's segment strategy: value, mid-market or premium. It positions a brand relative to others in the category. It is a statement of quality. It hints at the ingredients that have gone into the product. It creates desirability and implies exclusivity. At the high-price end of a category, it pays tribute to customers' lifestyles, tastes and collective discernment, as well as recognizes their purchasing power. It also gives customers entry into a club where high levels of sophistication, detailing and craftsmanship are defining attributes. On the other side of the price spectrum, at the economy end of a category, price is about inclusion, democratization and the trickling down of high-end benefits into lower-priced brands.

Brands thrive at both ends of the price spectrum. Take smartphones, for example. Chinese brands such as Oppo offer multiple models at the entry level of the market, helping customers with smaller wallets enter the category and remain in it. South Korea's Samsung straddles both ends of the spectrum, offering a range of phones at different price points, which allows the company to respond to demand at different price-quality points in the category. Samsung's phone prices typically range from just above Chinese brands to just below the industry's perceived quality leader Apple. (The iPhone, of course, sits at the very top of the market in terms of price, desirability and image.)

Arithmetically, a brand presents customers with a *value equation*: attributes, benefits, services and rewards in the numerator; price in the denominator. A positive value equation comes from the balance being in favour of the numerator. A high price is not in itself a disincentive, if the numerator has attractive features and benefits. An Apple is not the cheapest laptop or mobile phone by any stretch of the imagination. But Apple laptops are seen as good value by the millions of customers who buy them. Their combination of design, performance, features, aesthetics and 'brand cool' stacks the numerator well in excess of the price in the denominator. Other brands that are great value to their customers despite high prices are BMW, the Taj group of hotels and Anita Dongre, the Indian fashion brand. A low price is not in itself an attraction, especially if the features and benefits in the numerator are few, fail to excite or don't deliver. Discounts are ubiquitous on Amazon and in most cases offer exceptional value, but even a casual glance at the customer reviews section reveals that not every brand bought through Amazon provides a positive value equation despite the low prices. If a brand fails to satisfy customers for the primary reason it is bought for, it is poor value no matter how affordable it is.

Price is also a statement of brand confidence. The ability to hold price in the face of competition is a testament to a brand's appeal. It comes from belief in the brand's value equation. Brands that are poorly differentiated and have low-strength customer bonds quickly discount prices. While this might get them some tactical business advantage—for a period of time—in the medium to long term the negative consequences on brand image, quality and desirability are deeply corrosive. A brand that is struggling to maintain prices is likely to be a brand with a range of health issues, including poor quality, insufficient differentiation and weak customer bonds.

4. Service

Retail, hospitality and airline brands have made service central to their strategies. But they are not the only ones. In the twenty-first century, every brand has a service dimension. Service plays a role at every stage of the customer journey: pre-, at- and post-purchase. The human face of service has existed since time immemorial, but today service also has a technology face. In tech brands—and also in the technology interfaces of non-tech brands—the ease of use and quality of experience are not just about the product interface; these are also linked to *service*.

The purpose of pre-purchase service is to make a brand easy and exciting to discover. It is not just about being present where customers look for you but also about having a unique and attractive personality and voice. The automobile brand Mini has an irresistible legacy. They made having a small, affordable but slightly impractical car hip and cool. The Union Jack-wrapped Mini Cooper is an icon of '60s and '70s British culture. In its present-day, BMW-owned avatar, with the new owners introducing performance enhancements and modern styling, it remains an attractive alternative to the sensible family car, despite climbing up the price ladder to the luxury segment. What Mini hasn't lost through this transition is the rakishness, elan and exuberance so integral to its personality. For this brand, the owner-car relationship is all about the joy of being with each other, as well as about fun and pleasure. It is akin to that heady, if slightly improper, love affair which so many of us experience at least once in our lifetimes; it doesn't always last but while it does, it gives us the time of our lives. The videos on the Mini website, presenting five different Mini models, flow from this understanding. The urban Minis in the videos dart around city streets, taking corners arguably a little too sharply. The videos give us a sense of a big-city love affair, as if two people—the personified car and the owner—are holding hands and darting joyously down streets and around corners. This sort of presentation not only makes it easy for customers to discover Mini, but it does so in a way that complements Mini's personality, leading, of course, to further contact between prospective customers and the brand. What terrific pre-purchase brand service!

At-purchase service takes place in brand-controlled spaces, like showrooms, flagship stores and stores-within-stores, as well as through distributors, franchisees and various other partner stores. Where the brand controls the environment, it can detail and micromanage the service experience. A brand's ability to micromanage the service experience wanes as control is ceded to partners. Take the case of Levi's. In their own stores, Levi's creates their intended brand environment, offers a very wide product range and provides attention to customers that meets Levi's service aspiration. Conversations about how a particular pair of jeans looks on a customer, and trials, can be had in an atmosphere of the brand's making. However, when customers buy Levi's at branded space within a large department store, the Levi's environment is compromised in no small measure, and the quality of service is in the hands of the department store's employees. When Levi's products are ordered online and are delivered to people's homes, there is even less of a service environment. The pair fits well and is liked, or is returned. Brands need to care about all these purchase scenarios while trying to optimize the brand's service to the customer in each of them.

Then, of course, there is the important aspect of after-purchase service. The iPhone is an admirable product. Buying one at an Apple Store tends to be easy and enjoyable. But there are times when your iPhone needs looking after some months into its use. That's when you need to knock on the door of an Apple service centre. This can prove less than enjoyable, especially in India, and might well be Apple's Achilles' heel here. Even in big cities there is often only one official service centre, miles away from where you live. When you get to the centre, there is a long wait before your token number is called. If you are fortunate, your problem is fixed under warranty. If you're out of warranty and must pay for repair, it could be expensive. Apple products, like those of many other brands, are a delight when they are working faultlessly, but may prove vexing when they are not.

A brand that does a great job of aftersales service in India is Hyundai. Their service dealers have a widespread presence and more often than not within easy driving distance. Appointments are comfortably made over the phone. Service is prompt and efficient and, most importantly, it is available at a reasonable price. Aftersales calls ensure your visit has been satisfactory.

5. Impact on planet

Customers all over the world are increasingly attentive to the environmental impact of the brands they use. Ten to fifteen years ago, a brand's environmental profile was of interest to a small section of environmentally active customers. Today, an ever-growing segment of customers is making concerns related to a brand's 'impact on the planet' central to their purchase decision. What was formerly interesting peripheral information is now a powerful contributor to a brand's equity and attractiveness.

Over the last several decades, much has happened around the globe on this front. Brands like Tesla, Patagonia and Toms have built huge reputations, customer bases and market valuations through businesses that are essentially better for our planet. But even if we set those aside—for not every company has the opportunities Tesla and Toms had due to their origins and history—legislation and activism have created an atmosphere of greater self-regulation. Environment compliances for most industries have risen. Much of this has happened in developed countries but not without having a global impact. Western brands can no longer turn a blind eye to the practices of their suppliers in distant corners of the world. They have been made accountable for this by governments and customers. About a decade ago, Nike was accused of using child labour in the production of shoes, clothing and soccer balls in Pakistan and Cambodia. (Nike's manufacturing was subcontracted to third parties in those and other emerging countries.) Nike has minimum required age standards of eighteen years for the production of footwear and sixteen years for apparel and equipment, but rogue actions by a few subcontractors put Nike in a very difficult position. The brand had to admit to investigators that its minimum required age standards had been ignored or flouted. New processes to prevent such incidents were put in place to repair the damage to the brand's reputation. That said, this remains a very embarrassing episode in the history of a great brand.[1]

In India, similar changes have been slow to come. Brands typically get away with a lot more, or doing a lot less, depending on how you look at it. Despite some states, such as Maharashtra, passing legislation to ban certain kinds of plastics, there is overall far less pressure on brands from the government. Ideas like extended producer responsibility (EPR) are still very far from becoming mainstream or policy. The bulk of India's customers do not yet make a brand's planet impact important to their purchase decisions. While this is changing, slowly but surely, it is fair to say that any movement has been more an outcome of global forces than of India's domestic awareness and momentum.

The future lies in brands stepping ahead of legislation and voluntarily making the motto 'better for the planet' an integral part of their DNA. This will put them on the same page as customers, for whom the environment is increasingly a preference factor. Millennials already index above the rest

---

[1]   John H. Cushman Jr., 'INTERNATIONAL BUSINESS; Nike Pledges to End Child Labor and Apply U.S. Rules Abroad', *New York Times*, 13 May 1998, https://www.nytimes.com/1998/05/13/business/international-business-nike-pledges-to-end-child-labor-and-apply-us-rules-abroad.html

of the population on this point. The generation of customers after them, which is still in school, will be ahead of today's millennials when they reach the right age and can express their buying preferences. The time for Indian brands to get ahead of the curve is now. Many Western companies are showing the way. Under Nike's Reuse-A-Shoe programme, old trainers, of any brand, are shredded and reduced to rubber, foam, leather and textile components which are then turned into granules to make sports and playground surfaces. Similarly, MAC Cosmetics has a Back-to-MAC scheme to recycle packaging. Apple is refurbishing and reselling old MacBooks and iPhones.

But Unilever has gone one large step beyond all those, showing the way ahead in an admirable fashion. In late 2019, Unilever announced ambitious new commitments to reduce its plastic waste and help create a circular economy in plastics.[2] This has two objectives: first, to halve Unilever's use of virgin plastic by reducing its use of plastic packaging; and second, to help the company collect and process more plastic than it sells. Apart from its immediate impact on sentiment about Unilever's corporate citizenship, it lays the ground beautifully for customer preference in the years to come. The environmental dividend of today's actions is appreciated by tomorrow's customers.

---

[2] 'Unilever Announces Ambitious New Commitments for a Waste-Free World', Unilever.com, 7 October 2019, https://www.unilever.com/news/press-releases/2019/unilever-announces-ambitious-new-commitments-for-a-waste-free-world.html and 'Unilever's Position on Packaging and the Circular Economy', https://www.unilever.com/Images/packaging-and-the-circular-economy-position-statement_tcm244-423161_en.pdf

6. Culture

'Your brand is your culture; your culture is your brand.' There's a resonant truth in this frequently heard observation. So much of a brand—or, as some argue, all of it—has to do with the people who work for it. They bring a range of intellects, imaginations and energies to a brand, and the alchemy of success results from this fusion between a brand and its people.

In today's times, when differentiation is so hard to find, a brand's people are key to its success. Stories of the online retailer Zappos' dedication to its customers are legendary; their phone service advisers are known for guiding customers through their purchases with seemingly endless patience.

The Merriam-Webster Dictionary defines culture as a 'set of shared attitudes, values, goals, and practices that characterizes an institution or organization'. Wikipedia tells us that 'organizational culture encompasses values and behaviours that contribute to the unique social and psychological environment of a business'.

These definitions are correct, of course. But brand culture is much more than that; it is the invisible glue that binds an organization together. It is not easy to distil into a set of words, and it is equally difficult to preserve, both in good times (as success brings growth) and in difficult times (leading to organizational changes). Yet, this invisible element makes such tremendous impact.

Brand culture has become a defining attribute of brands and a preference creator not only in the battle for customers but also in the race for recruiting top talent. What attracts the brightest and best to work somewhere? Culture. It is what candidates ask about; it is what recruiters pitch; it is what a walk-through of a brand's premises reveals glimpses of. What are the things an organization holds in high esteem? What will it do and not do? How will it create workplaces? How does it spark creativity and group work? How does it look at career advancement? How do leaders speak with staff? How does information travel through the company? What attitudes guide the behaviour towards women? What policies are in place to handle unsavoury situations like sexual harassment, should they arise? What diversity policies and practices are in place? All these and other aspects of culture define the brand. They also strongly determine how the brand is perceived by customers, because a company that treats its people well more often than not creates a brand that treats customers well.

While there are infinite variations in corporate culture, it is rare to find a hugely successful brand with unhappy people behind it. Some, of course, exist, but they are few and far between and likely to be in categories where the number of brands and extent of differentiation have not reached critical levels. The moment critical levels are reached, brands with great leadership, happy people and vibrant workplaces will pull away from those with tyrannical or autocratic leaders, employees who hate Mondays and pre-Industrial Revolution workplaces.

Culture is an essential differentiator for twenty-first-century brands. The best brand cultures put the customer at the centre of their purpose. Its people are excited to meet customers, to find ways to delight them and to make customers' interactions with the brand pleasurable and rewarding.

Global brands with service interfaces—such as McDonald's—have business models that extend across geography and languages. A McDonald's restaurant looks the same in every part of the world, the food is more or less the same everywhere (allowing, of course, for obvious differences in palate and diet), as is the greeting and service you receive. McDonald's has largely made their service independent of the individuals who provide it in Mumbai, Miami or Manchester, by reducing all operations to simple reproducible processes that everyone must unfailingly adhere to. We see similar 'service as a process' models in many other global brands, especially in the hospitality and aviation sectors. And yet, why is it that you feel just a bit more welcome and better looked after at some McDonald's branch or Marriott property or Singapore Airlines flight than at others? Why does the smile on the face and the ring in the voice feel genuine in some instances and not in others? That's because the interpretation of brand culture by that particular McDonald's store manager or that Marriott general manager or that Singapore Airlines flight services leader has created a 'people chemistry' among her team, and that's what makes for tangibly better service.

7. Storytelling

Brands have always told stories, some true, others less so. Advertising is, after all, said to be the second oldest profession. It is easy to imagine ancient times, when these stories were told orally, in markets and bazaars, by those who had a loud voice and a smooth tongue, extolling the virtues of one product over another, explicating why one craftsman's wares were superior to the identical ones in the neighbouring store. Then came the printing press and with it handbills, newspaper ads and posters. Cinema and television ushered in the thirty-second-long advertisement, which is still in vogue. And in the present day, social media is added to the mix, to tell newer and better brand stories.

While brand stories have existed since time immemorial, brand storytelling has become a buzzword only in recent times. Contemporary brand and marketing gurus make a powerful argument that without great storytelling, brands are nowhere. And right they are. Except that the idea of brand storytelling is not new. What is new is to whom we tell these stories, where we tell them and what we hear back about them.

Digital technology has put Poseidon's trident in every marketer's hand. The first prong is data: reading the digital footprints customers leave through their app and social media usage and online buying. This is telling marketers more about their audiences than ever before. The second is social media, which gives brands the platforms to participate in customer conversations about a range of interests and current affairs. The third, every marketer's dream: the ability to personalize marketing messages. It is empowering for a marketer to be able to have many million individual conversations simultaneously. In the past, they could have a complex conversation with a few people in person or, through media like television, have a simple conversation with many millions. Now, with the help of AI, you can have individual conversations on a mass scale.

For the twenty-first-century brand, storytelling offers never before seen opportunities, but also never before seen challenges. The opportunity is to use different aspects of a brand's story to appeal to a range of customer motivations and interests at different points in the customer journey. The challenge is to do this in an interesting manner, across touchpoints, so that customers don't feel stalked or over-marketed to. This is a large enough topic to devote an entire chapter to (Chapter 7, 'How to Talk to People').

8. Customer experience

Steve Jobs once made a wonderful—and widely quoted—point about customer experience: 'You've got to start with the customer experience and work backwards to the technology—you can't start with the technology and try to figure out where you're going to try to sell it.'

That pretty much says it all about the centrality of customer experience to brands, doesn't it?

Customer experience is the net impression a brand creates with a customer, across every stage of the customer journey, in all the many contact points between brand and customer, through the entire length of the business relationship. It is seen by most leading brands as the #1 brand differentiator in the 2020s.

Customers are extremely sensitive to their experiences with a brand. Many leave a brand after just one bad experience. Brands that manage the customer experience well often command premiums over like-to-like competition. Great customer experience creates strong customer bonds. It builds relationships, loyalty, positive word-of-mouth publicity and good customer reviews.

Some customer journeys are short and low-risk. You feel like eating potato chips, you walk to the nearest store, buy a packet, eat the chips, and dispose of the empty packet (hopefully in a recycle bin). The bulk of the brand experience lies in the product being available and tasting good. While the potato crisps customer journey is short and frequently repeated, other journeys are long and high-risk. For example, admitting a three-year-old to school. The child will be there for several years. Choosing the wrong school could have many unattractive downstream consequences. Obviously, parents will participate in a long and complex evaluation of their options. Each school will make a case for why it's the best. After the child is admitted, the school embarks on a many-year journey to help the child discover the fullness of her potential. Managing the entire customer journey to maximize parent satisfaction is not just vital for the child already in school, it becomes an important factor for parents looking to admit younger children to a school. Beyond that, the school-child-parent covenant is also a moral and social responsibility for the brand.

There is a question well worth asking about brands: When someone is narrating a personal story of importance from their lives—like a holiday, a difficult hospitalization or a crisis on a business trip—will the brand feature favourably in it? If such a narration isn't complete without mention of the stellar part played by a brand in it, then the brand has done an admirable job in creating a great customer experience.

There you have it: the Brand Octagon for the authentic twenty-first-century brand. Are many Indian brands on this path, with all eight sides of the octagon defining them? How does one go about putting one's brand on this path? Let's look at this in the next chapter.

VI

Where Are Brands Going?

Nugget 6: How to Craft an Authentic Brand

'I saw the angel in the marble and carved until I set him free.'

—Michelangelo

In the previous chapter, I revealed a definitive brand principle for the 2020s: authenticity. Authentic brands find favour with customers today and will increasingly do so as the decade unfolds. To achieve authenticity, the Brand Octagon is my recommended model.

So how do you go about creating your authentic brand? What ideas and practices feed into the Brand Octagon? There are two pools of 'genetic material' that help you add content to your Brand Octagon and define your brand.

Pools of Brand DNA	
VISIBLE DNA	**INVISIBLE DNA**
Product	History
Packaging	Vision
Pricing	Mission
Presence	Purpose
Personality	Values
Brand identity	People
Content	Culture
Media	Competencies

On one side we have the 'Invisible DNA', consisting of eight strands: history, vision, mission, purpose, values, people, culture and competencies. My use of the word 'invisible' for them should not suggest in any way that they are less important. On the contrary, they are extremely important and potent, in fact crucial, for an authentic brand. I refer to them as invisible only because they aren't directly seen or experienced by customers; they are seen and experienced through a brand's 'Visible DNA'. All the eight strands are powerful individually and, working in synergy with each other, play a seminal role in shaping a brand.

On the other side we have the 'Visible DNA', also consisting of eight strands: product, packaging, pricing, presence, personality, visual identity, content and media. These are the identifiers that customers see and base their purchase choices on. This list of eight items, which gets continuous attention in the daily management of brands, is familiar to most marketers.

The two pools of DNA are not separated by a wall or moat. On the contrary, they are co-dependent and interlinked.

When the eight strands of Invisible DNA are crystal clear and inspiringly articulated, it makes a brand sharply defined. When the Visible DNA is successful in creating attention, engagement and sales, it adds value to the Invisible DNA, and helps new vision and ambitions spring forth.

Some brands choose to make an element of their Invisible DNA—e.g. purpose—visible to customer and other stakeholder audiences. This might be permanent or for a short period of time, targeting all audiences or a selection. Sometimes a brand chooses to tactically suppress or modify an element of its Visible DNA—e.g. personality—when faced with negative media coverage or other adverse conditions.

Invisible DNA

1. *History*

For many a young person, history has little appeal. The clock starts now and the direction to look in is ahead. The view through the windshield, or even the side windows, is more exciting than the one in the rear-view mirror.

This is true of every new generation of marketers.

When young marketers start on a brand, the more astute among them will look into its history, especially if the brand has a long and storied past that has been thoroughly documented and catalogued. (This, sadly, is not always the case.) Looking into your brand's history is like looking at an old family album. It shows where you come from and what made you who you are. It contains stories about your forebears, replete with their amusing, idiosyncratic and brave doings. It weaves a rich tapestry, and brings detail and character to the family legend.

Brand history is not just a collection of interesting episodes; it provides vital continuity. Why was a new brand idea created in 1996? Why was an identity refresh done in 2005? How did a particular manager, now retired, put a strategy in place for modern trade in 2010? How did a predecessor deal with the onslaught of online retail in 2015? Past brand managers would have dealt with a range of issues, echoes of which might still be heard in the present. Brand history is not just optional reading; it gives marketers the bedrock on which to build the brand's future. Successive brand managers add their own chapters to the pages of brand history, for future marketers to admire and benefit from.

An example of a brand that found a future strategy in its past is Kentucky Fried Chicken. In 1975, KFC discontinued the use of images of its iconic founder, Colonel Sanders, in their marketing campaigns, a practice that had lasted for over forty years. The company had suffered nearly a decade of declining sales when they hired the advertising agency Wieden+Kennedy in 2015. To turn things around, W+K recommitted KFC to what had made the company special in the first place: its founder, Colonel Sanders, and his values.[1]

So they brought back the Colonel. Images of this ultimate chicken salesman began appearing in unexpected places in pop culture, like at Comic-Con events (as well as in comic books made by DC Comics), in romance novels

---

[1] 'KFC: The Return of the Colonel', WK.com, August 2017, https://www.wk.com/work/kfc-the-return-of-the-colonel/

(with KFC's very own book, *Tender Wings of Desire*), as part of the conversation around AI (with the HARLAND robot) and even on KFC Limited, an online store with merchandising.

In 2017, they took their campaign to new heights, literally and figuratively. In one of the biggest earned-media moments of the year, KFC sent its new Zinger chicken sandwich to the edge of space, in partnership with aerospace company World View. To demonstrate how to make 'Original Recipe' fried chicken—and help recruit and train cooks—they created an immersive VR game, produced entirely in-house. Last but not least, in one of the most talked-about social stunts, they quietly followed six men named Herb and all five Spice Girls on Twitter in a nod to KFC's secret eleven herbs and spices recipe. The move garnered over 2 billion earned impressions, appearing everywhere from the *Today Show* to the front page of Reddit.

Finally, KFC was back in the cultural conversation, with *Eater* magazine giving its #Brand of the Year award to KFC, and the Colonel appearing organically in shows like *Curb Your Enthusiasm*. Best of all, KFC's campaign helped drive four years of same-store sales growth. For Kentucky Fried Chicken, things are once again 'finger lickin' good'.[2]

In encouraging you to delve into a brand's history, I am not suggesting that all the answers for the future lie in the past. Of course they don't. The approach should be, 'Learn from the past, excel in the present, invent for the future.'

---

[2]   Greg Morabito, 'KFC Is Eater's #Brand of the Year', *Eater*, 5 December 2017, https://www.eater.com/2017/12/5/16390270/kfc-ads-brand-of-the-year-eater-awards-2017

2. *Vision*

A clearly articulated company vision is scintillating and inspiring. (It is the opposite when written without clarity or in language dull as ditchwater.) A well-written vision acts like Polaris, guiding the passage of the brand ship, laden with valuable cargo, on uncharted seas and bringing it into port.

Satya Nadella's impact on Microsoft is the stuff of dreams. Under his leadership over the past six years, Microsoft's performance has been transformed on pretty much every business metric. Its top line has risen by 50 per cent, to $125 billion, and valuation threefold, to a trillion dollars.

In 2017, three years into Nadella's tenure, Microsoft rearticulated its vision. Here is a selection from Microsoft's 2017 vision statement:

> Microsoft is a technology company whose mission is to empower every person and every organization on the planet to achieve more. We strive to create local opportunity, growth, and impact in every country around the world. Our strategy is to build best-in-class platforms and productivity services for an intelligent cloud and an intelligent edge infused with artificial intelligence ('AI').[3]

Here's what their preceding vision statement, from 2016, had said:

---

[3]   Nat Levy, 'Microsoft's Bew Corporate Vision: Artificial Intelligence Is In and Mobile Is Out', *GeekWire*, 2 August 2017, https://www.geekwire.com/2017/microsofts-new-corporate-vision-artificial-intelligence-mobile/

Microsoft is a technology company whose mission is to empower every person and every organization on the planet to achieve more. Our strategy is to build best-in-class platforms and productivity services for a mobile-first, cloud-first world . . . The mobile-first, cloud-first world is transforming the way individuals and organizations use and interact with technology.[4]

Comparing those statements, three things become clear:

1. Microsoft *stuck by* its vision to empower every person and organization.
2. What it changed was its strategy on how to do that. It went from 'mobile-first, cloud-first' to 'intelligent cloud . . . and AI'. In other words: increased focus on cloud; mobile out, AI in.
3. 'Local . . . impact in every country in the world' gets a prominent place in the 2017 vision.

No surprise, then, that Microsoft's cloud business was a significant contributor to its 2018 top line.

Its 2017 vision defines Microsoft's path to growth sharply and unambiguously for employees, customers and associates. The core of the Microsoft brand becomes so clear to see because of its articulate, precise and simple vision statement.

---

[4]   Ibid.

3. *Mission*

In June 2017, Mark Zuckerberg spoke at the first-ever Facebook Community Summit:

> For the past 10 years, our mission has been to make the world more open and connected. We will always work to give people a voice and help us stay connected, but now we will do even more. Today, we're expanding our mission to set our course for the next 10 years.
>
> The idea for our new mission is: 'bring the world closer together'.
>
> Our full mission statement is: give people the power to build community and bring the world closer together. That reflects that we can't do this ourselves, but only by empowering people to build communities and bring people together.[5]

The clarity of Facebook's mission defines the brand and its strategy for the next ten years. It explains to all stakeholders what the brand is about and what it wants to achieve.

To conclude with another example, here's Khan Academy's mission statement: 'Our mission is to provide a free, world-class education for everyone, everywhere.' How simple and clear that statement is. Although 'mission' is a strand of the brand DNA not visible to most customers, the Visible DNA of brand Khan Academy will fully embody

---

[5]   Mark Zuckerberg, 'Bringing the World Closer Together', Facebook.com, 22 June 2017, https://www.facebook.com/notes/mark-zuckerberg/bringing-the-world-closer-together/10154944663901634/

its mission: free (price); world-class (product); everyone, everywhere (presence).

4. *Purpose*

Brand purpose is the reason for the brand to exist beyond making money. A simple yet powerful idea. But also controversial. As with many powerful ideas, 'you either love it or hate it' (to borrow a line from Marmite's legendary advertising campaign).

Richard Shotton, consultant and author of *The Choice Factory*, and formerly head of behavioural science at Manning Gottlieb OMD, is not a believer. In a 2018 article for *Campaign* magazine, Shotton wrote:

> The most quoted evidence supporting brand purpose comes from *Grow*, a book written by Jim Stengel, ex-CMO of P&G. Stengel came up with this finding after selecting the 50 brands with the highest loyalty or bonding scores from Millward Brown's 50,000-strong database.
>
> These star performers were termed the Stengel 50. Stengel then searched for a link between the brands. This was found to be a brand ideal . . .
>
> Next, he looked at the chosen brands' stock value growth between 2000 and 2011. Stengel 50 had grown by 382 percent . . . he declared that ideals were driving business success.[6]

---

6   Richard Shotton, 'Book Review: Flawed Evidence for Brand Purpose', *Campaign,* 23 October 2018, https://www.campaignlive.co.uk/article/book-review-flawed-evidence-brand-purpose/1496998

While acknowledging that Stengel's book has had tremendous impact, Shotton is convinced that Stengel's evidence is flawed. He questions the conclusions on four points: 1) Is the data accurate? 2) Does the theory predict the future as well as the past? 3) Are the brands linked by an ideal? 4) Do brands with ideals outperform those without?

Another practitioner who questions brand purpose is Ipsos's Samira Brophy. In her 2017 article 'Brand Purpose: What's the Point of You?', Brophy writes:

> Every brand study in my research career has pointed to purpose being a weak driver of equity. Consumers would like companies to be ethical on their behalf, but will not go out of their way to choose differently if a product has an important function in their lives. Therefore, a humbler and more commercially oriented view would be to play a purposeful part in people's real lives. Which is traditionally good positioning practice. Without good positioning, a stratospheric cause can amount to very little brand impact.[7]

Brophy's lead point: people will choose a good product over a good cause.

Stengel's own Jim Stengel Company website is, unsurprisingly, pro-purpose. He uses multiple sources to underline the power of purpose, and refers to it often in his *The CMO Podcast*.

---

7   Samira Brophy, 'Brand Purpose: What's the Point of You?', Ipsos.com, 1 December 2017, https://www.ipsos.com/en/brand-purpose-whats-point-you

In summary, points 1 to 4 of the Invisible DNA help to articulate the core of the Brand Octagon. They help a marketer answer the three questions that define the core of your brand: Why are you here? What do you do? How do you do it?

5. Values

Personal values are what we believe strongly in and hold sacrosanct. They are the guiding principles for our decisions and actions. They determine how we behave and how we would like others to behave with us. Personal values, not just of leaders but of every person in the company, shape the organization. They shape the values of the organization's brands. And, in return, organization and brand values shape personal values on a range of issues including diversity in the workforce, respect for women and scrupulous corporate governance.

In 2019, the global co-working brand WeWork made headlines for the implosion of its highly anticipated initial public offering (IPO). From a peak valuation of $47 billion, WeWork was revalued at $8 billion. Its lead strategic investor SoftBank stepped in with additional funding on the condition that WeWork co-founder and CEO Adam Neumann leave the company. As more news reports on this issue surfaced, it became clear that underlying the financial meltdown was a distressing story of WeWork's organizational values and Neumann's (and his close associates') personal values. Media coverage alleged that the founders had misused their position of privilege and that they illegally carried restricted substances across international borders, sexually harassed women, and were responsible for poor corporate governance and bad investment and acquisition strategies.[8]

In a nutshell, questionable personal values leading to questionable corporate values. Will this affect the attractiveness of the WeWork brand? Will revenue-bringing current members of the WeWork community choose an alternative co-working space on account of the reputation damage to WeWork? Will potential members remove WeWork from their consideration set and choose another co-working brand instead? Customers, both present and future, will make their own calls, but one thing is clear: WeWork's reputation is greatly dented. Customers might well be asking themselves whether their rental payments would have been lower had WeWork's leadership espoused better values. The brand has lost its gloss. Its status has gone from unicorn to question mark. The new team at WeWork has work to do to restore their brand's values.

Raymond is an Indian textile and apparel brand. Founded in 1925 and 'guide to the well-dressed male' for nearly a century, Raymond continues to stand tall in the men's formal wear sector. The brand is gentlemanly and stylish, if a little formal. It targets affluent Indian men, helping them explore new looks, new products and new experiences, making every occasion special. Raymond expresses its values and beliefs as, 'We care for excellence in everything we do.' This helps define the brand and translates to the quality of their textiles, the look and feel

---

8   Matthew Zeitlin, 'Why WeWork Went Wrong', *Guardian*, 20 December 2019, https://www.theguardian.com/business/2019/dec/20/why-wework-went-wrong

of their flagship stores and the products offered in them, Raymond's bespoke made-to-measure business and a range of other activities. The 'caring for excellence' value drives conversations within the organization and behaviour with customers.

6. People

'A company's best assets ride up in the elevator every morning, and ride down every night.' The old chestnut is as true today as when it was invented.

The memorable moments brands want to create and share with their customers are imagined, designed and delivered by people. AI is playing an increasingly important role in certain kinds of experience delivery, and perhaps the day is not far away when AI will replace or convincingly simulate human interaction. But for the moment, brands are about people.

At a certain point in my career, I was based in London, in a global role at the marketing services company J. Walter Thompson, handling their client Unilever. I travelled often, and long distances, with Japan being a frequent destination. I would fly Virgin Atlantic to Tokyo, principally on account of their excellent service and the little extras, like a limousine drop to and from the airport. On one such two-day visit to Tokyo, the flight attendant looking after my section served my favourite Virgin Mary after take-off. (I had stopped drinking alcohol on flights by this time, experience having taught me that I arrived at my destination in better shape without it.) Two days later, on my return Virgin flight to

London, in a remarkable double coincidence, I was in
the same seat I'd occupied on the flight to Tokyo and the
same flight attendant was serving my section again. To my
delight, not only did she greet me by name, she went on to
spontaneously add, 'Mr Bambawale, I'll bring your Virgin
Mary as soon as the captain turns off the seat belts sign.'
Service beyond the call of duty, delivered by an inspired
member of the brand team, taking my admiration for Virgin
to an even higher level. I never had a repeat experience on
subsequent Virgin flights, but that quick-thinking flight
attendant made sure I never flew another airline on any
sector where Virgin had a flight.

People make the difference. People who fit together help
brands grow; those who don't, damage or destroy brands.
Hiring great people across the entire company is central to
building great brands.

Great brands are not made by committees; they are
made by great marketers who are clever, intuitive and brave.
They don't always work in the marketing team or have the
initialism 'CMO' below the names on their business cards.
Sunil Mittal, chairman of Bharti Enterprises, my boss for
two years when I was the global brand director of Bharti
Airtel, is one of the finest natural marketers I have had
the privilege to work with. Sunil's innate marketing savvy
is remarkable and his instincts sound. I would see Sunil
for regular brand catch-ups. He would instantly 'get' the
brand programmes I was updating him on. A short while
later, I had his perspective and he had mine; we concurred,
and another programme that elevated the Airtel brand was
under way.

7. *Culture*

Colloquially, culture is 'How we do things here'. It refers to what is individually and collectively valued, how people interact and behave with each other and with external stakeholders, what is rewarded and celebrated, what is unacceptable and rejected.

While most corporate cultures are about setting up social guard rails, it is the unwritten codes that act as the real social glue. Cultures that are open, democratic, supportive of innovation and publicly celebrate achievements are the promoters of creativity and teamwork. Cultures that are wheels within wheels, with secret coteries and shadowy inner circles, where a single leader makes unilateral decisions, are likely to promote individualism and protectionism.

Corporate cultures affect brands deeply because they have a direct impact on how teams work together and on their attitudes towards customers. How does a brand approach the challenge of satisfying customers' needs? Are customer relationships about commitment and care, or are they purely about profit? Can a brand thrive in the elder-care industry, for example, driven only by profit? Will seniors be treated with respect and with their dignity preserved, or will they be treated as 'inmates'? Will a senior citizen living on his own in a retirement community be denied emergency care because the package he has bought does not cover some services? These are just some of the concerns linked to customer decisions wherein the culture of the organization plays a significant role.

Points 5 to 7 of the Invisible DNA contribute to articulating the service, impact on planet, culture and customer experience sides of the Brand Octagon.

8. Competencies

A professor opened a class in my first week in business school with a question that has stayed with me my entire life and become something of a personal mantra: *'What do you know that others don't?'*

This pretty much says it all, doesn't it? It could be a poster on every wall in every office in every corporation. The monetization of the things you know (and others don't) creates a business.

In my career I've discovered there are corollaries to that question. What are the things you do better than others? Will others want to know and do those things? What do you want from others in exchange for sharing with them the things you know?

Competencies are the things you know and do well, ideally better than others. Unique competencies are hard to come by, so when you have them you need to protect and nurture them, no matter which area you operate in and what kind of organization you have. Competencies lead you to deliver performance to customers on attributes that are important to them. They guide product development, pricing decisions and how you communicate your brand's story.

'The things you know and do well' need to be updated and upgraded with changing times, or you face the risk of your brand failing to compete. Take the case of FedEx.

Not too long ago, very few brands, if any, could deliver a parcel on time better than FedEx. The brand was synonymous with the category: you 'FedEx-ed' parcels. Then, along came Amazon, which became one of FedEx's largest customers. As the Amazon business grew manifold, FedEx—whose core competency, due to its origin, lay in delivering parcels to businesses—found itself struggling to master on-time delivery of packages to homes. Amazon developed this competency themselves, so much so that in Christmas 2019 in the USA, Amazon delivery vans seemed to be perpetually visible in residential neighbourhoods, against a rare FedEx one. Since Amazon took their business away, FedEx has been struggling and its stock price is on the decline. FedEx urgently needs to discover and master a new competency, relevant to the times, to survive as a delivery brand.[9]

In urban India, Swiggy is a leading food delivery brand. A Swiggy delivery man zipping by on a scooter is a common sight. What's not that well known is that outside food delivery, Swiggy adds revenue through other kinds of delivery services. If you want to send an envelope to your brother on the other side of town, Swiggy will deliver it for you. Extending a competency—from food delivery to the delivery of small parcels—is a natural move into an adjacent space. But it also makes Swiggy a challenger to local couriers, who will need to up their game to remain competitive.

---

[9]   Jon Markman, 'Amazon Vs. FedEx: From Colleagues to Competitors', *Forbes*, 15 January 2020, https://www.forbes.com/sites/jonmarkman/2020/01/15/amazon-vs-fedex-from-colleagues-to-competitors/#71c1f78d6778

Point 8 of the Invisible DNA—competencies—contributes to the performance, product interface, pricing and storytelling sides of the Brand Octagon.

Visible DNA

1. Product

Products create outcomes; brands create relationships. Products fulfil category needs; brands fulfil the human needs that sit above categories.

Suppose a man wants to hang a beautiful painting on a wall in his home. The products he needs are a drill, tape measure, spirit level, hammer or screwdriver, pencil, drywall anchor and a nail or screw. To create the desired outcome, the tape needs to measure accurately, the pencil make a tidy mark, the drill a sharp hole, the anchor fit that hole perfectly and the nail or screw sit neatly in it. Once the painting is hung, the spirit level must confirm it is stable and aligned. Let's further suppose that every tool the man uses does its job perfectly and the painting hangs just as it should. All the products have done what was expected of them well.

But when one or another of the products in that list steps beyond its specific task to participate in the overarching human need, it starts to become a brand. Let's say it's the drill, a Black & Decker. Now, Black & Decker takes the trouble to find out *which* painting the man in hanging on the wall. B&D discovers that the painting was done by the man's ten-year-old daughter. It is a sign that her talent in art is extraordinary.

That painting now has a special significance. It being on the wall is not just about its beauty; it is about the talent of a child and the love of a father (relating to the *connection, joy of ownership* and *value-added experiences* motivators and the *personality* influencer in my customer motivation model in Section 1). If Black & Decker were to weave this into their conversation with customers, they start to participate in the human needs that sit above the category needs. By elevating their participation in the customer's life, they are on the path to becoming a brand.

Great products can succeed without being great brands. But rarely, if ever, is the opposite true: a successful brand that doesn't have a great product. The Indian telecom major Jio is an example of the former: it is essentially an attractively priced product which meets the category need. Whether Jio participates at the human-needs level remains a question.

Conversely, Vodafone in India is an example of a great brand that was once a great product. But after the merger with former competitor Idea, it mystifyingly lost its way. Product performance slumped, leading to a mass exodus of customers. From being India's foremost telecom brand just half a decade ago, with strong market shares built on good data packages, a reliable network and engaging communication, Vodafone is now gasping for life.

You cannot be a great brand without being a great product. Customers will not give you permission to have a larger human conversation with them without you excelling at category needs. This is why product is the primary strand of a brand's Visible DNA.

2. *Packaging*

Packaging is prime brand real estate. Subject to regulations (and good taste), you can pretty much put anything you like on it. If your product is 'anonymous'—like tea, water, an Indian spice or petrol—there's only so much you can do to the product in terms of visible product differentiation. Packaging becomes the avenue to make a first-level visible difference while moving up the value chain from commodity.

Indians have a huge appetite for local snacks. Samosas, kachoris, papads, sevs and gulab jamuns are only a few that figure on that seemingly endless list. The first choice of the hungry or the bored is of course the fresh-made snack, whether delivered by the favourite neighbourhood chaat wallah or made at home by a family member. But with changing lifestyles and the growth of the processed food industry, the packaged Indian snacks category has exploded. Many FMCG majors have brands in this segment, PepsiCo with Kurkure and ITC with Bingo among them. Giving them a run for their money, and often beating them at their own game, are Indian brands Haldiram's, Bikaji, and Balaji Wafers.

Haldiram's is a packaging success story. Starting from a single shop in Bikaner in 1937, the brand is now valued at $3 billion. It was reported in 2019 that Kellogg's was interested in a buy-in.[10] Haldiram's popular *bhujia* is complemented by

---

[10] Chitranjan Kumar, 'Kellogg's Goes Beyond Breakfast, Seeks Snacky Bites of Halidram's', *Business Today*, 14 February 2019, https://www.businesstoday.in/current/corporate/kellogg-goes-beyond-breakfast-seeks-snacky-bites-of-halidram/story/318712.html

a range of packaged Indian snacks, and their products are available not just in grocery stores across the country but also in impressive Haldiram's stores at airports. Their expertise lies in offering popular Indian snacks in packaged form *without making more than an acceptable compromise on the expected taste.* The fresh snack remains the gold standard, but when that is not available Haldiram's is the number-one alternative.

In the shampoo segment in India, a well-documented contributor to growth is the sachet category. These single-use shampoo packets have expanded the market considerably. (That they have created an environmental nuisance alongside, since the triple-layer plastic they are made from is non-biodegradable, is another matter.) Looking at sachets purely from a marketing point of view, they are singularly responsible for the success of Cavinkare's CHIK shampoo.

How a brand uses this very visible strand of its DNA, the prime real estate of its packaging, is a significant contributor to its success.

3. *Pricing*

I've looked at price from a number of points of view in the previous chapter. So I won't go over those again here.

Customers generally accept that something that is of high quality will be more expensive to buy. Strong brands use price to make the perceived value many times more than the cost or quality. Take the fashion industry, where even prêt-à-porter sees markups of 300–400 per cent, sometimes more. What is the delivered cost of a Gucci handbag, a Louis Vuitton suitcase or a Burberry coat? A fraction of the price the customer pays.

The difference between the price a customer is happy to pay and the total cost at point of purchase is the value added by branding. Marketers can increase this value manifold. That's the point of branding: making a commodity more valuable for both company and customer. That's why price is such an important element of the Visible DNA.

4. *Presence*

Availability—distribution, if you like—is undoubtedly a key aspect of presence. Being present where customers are buying, when they are buying, after they have bought.

But the idea of brand presence is larger than that.

Great brands achieve a desirable ubiquity. They are welcomed into areas of the customer's world where products are not allowed. Customers give the brands they like and hold in high esteem permission to participate in their social conversations, about the things that matter to them. This expands a brand's presence beyond points of purchase, from a transactional to a participative role.

Within the larger space of child-rearing, education is close to parents' hearts. They are always interested in information and news that can be of help in this regard. How can moms and dads help their children manage exam stress? How should they deal with peer pressure and bullying? How can high academic achievers become all-rounders? How can low academic achievers perform better? There are many such questions and the list is endless. An education brand can significantly expand its authority by participating in conversations about these questions and bringing new perspectives. Customers will open doors to a brand that does this, choosing it over its competitors. This is what brand presence can do.

Customers show their approval of a brand that has a noticeable presence through positive social comments and by sharing branded content. Brands that achieve a high level of invited participation in customers' lives immunize themselves from the ups and downs of a transactional relationship.

5. *Personality*

In Bollywood's current pantheon of male stars, the heaviest hitters are the three Khans: Aamir, Salman and Shah Rukh. At one level, they have so much in common: they're all in their fifties, have a string of big hits to their names, give any movie they are in a massive opening weekend and have earned the film business a lot of money at the box office. Each also has a production company, and is immensely successful and very wealthy. But beyond this superficial similarity, they are very different people.

Aamir Khan is a thinking man's star. He chooses his roles carefully, works on one film at a time, participates behind the scenes in the films he is in to a considerable degree and has a gift for turning stories with a social message into blockbusters that appeal to audiences everywhere. Aamir was also the heart and soul—and presenter—of a social responsibility TV show called *Satyamev Jayate*. His films are hugely popular in China, where he is a megastar.

Salman Khan is the common man's rugged action star. His films are pitched to small-town and rural audiences (not that they don't do well in big cities). The characters he plays are rough around the edges—tough guys or simpletons but always with a heart of gold under a brawling exterior. Salman has been hosting, in characteristic style, the reality show *Bigg Boss* (an Indian take on *Big Brother*) since its fourth season in 2011.

Shah Rukh Khan is the eternal romantic star, whom audiences—especially women—adore, even when he (very rarely) doesn't get the girl at the end of a film. He also does action movies well. Unlike Aamir and Salman, he does not come from a film family and made it in Bollywood on his own. He is sweet, charming, friendly, grateful for the attention he gets, gracious with fans and so hugely popular that people often throng the street outside his home hoping for a glimpse of him. On TV, Shah Rukh has hosted *Kaun Banega Crorepati* and *TED Talks India Nayi Soch*, a show based on the TED format.

The point is about personality: Aamir, the intellectual; Salman, the rugged; Shah Rukh, the romantic.

As it is with the three Khans, so it is with brands. Great brands have unique personalities that set them apart from the other brands in their category. Back when Vodafone was thriving in India, it had a young, slightly irreverent personality that made it very popular with youth, pushing Airtel and Idea into older profiles. Today, with Vodafone Idea in a terminal tailspin and a monolithic Jio, the opportunity to carve a distinct personality rests with Airtel. What Airtel will make of this opportunity remains to be seen.

Personality is critical to differentiation and arguably the most powerful strand of the Visible DNA. It is what makes a brand interesting to audiences.

6. *Visual identity*

Logo. Typography. Colour palette. Tag line. Photo style. Illustration style.

There are so many elements to the visual identity of a brand. At the most obvious level, the visual identity ensures recognition. At an advanced level it evokes brand associations built over time or through other elements of the brand's communication strategy. One level beyond that, a brand's visual identity can trigger demand. For example, a Burger King sign might remind you of being hungry or entice you to have a snack even when you weren't thinking of having it.

While visual identity provides the primary recognition to a brand, there are other identifiers as well, such as audio, olfactory, tactile and product design identifiers. A BMW car door shuts with a reassuring thunk, conveying strength. Odomos has a citrus aroma that you can recognize instantly. Marmite's taste is unmistakable. The elegant lines of an Apple laptop are unique.

Great brands turn elements of their visual identities into powerful symbols of what they stand for. The golden arches of McDonald's are legendary, as are the classic contours of the Coke bottle and of Shell's seashell emblem. The same

can be said about the other identifiers of these brands, like
typography, palette and tag line.

7. *Content*

Arguably the most compelling strand of a brand's DNA is
its communication model. Brands that put out engaging
communication receive a disproportionate share of customer
attention.

Today, with so much content out there and so many
distractions for customers, getting their attention and having
them spend time with a brand is a huge challenge. Brands
that meet this challenge typically seize a higher share of the
customer demand.

Central to communication is brand voice and point of
view. The voice in which a brand speaks—authoritative,
friendly, self-deprecating, conspiring, etc.—and its point
of view on topics important for its customers determine
the efficacy of its communication strategy. Take the ice
cream brand Ben & Jerry's. Their flavour names—Gimme
S'more, Cherry Garcia, The Tonight Dough, Americone
Dream and so on—are a pleasure to discover. Their website
is refreshing to look at. Their three-part mission statement
is easy to read and understand. Ben & Jerry's brand
voice is light, amusing and ebullient. Their point of view
could be translated thus: make the world a better place and
enjoy yourself while doing so. This is a brand that does not
take itself too seriously.

Content is so important for brand building that I have
devoted the entire next chapter to it. Jump ahead if you like,

though I would have you stay with me through the rest of this chapter.

8. *Media*

It is a long-established practice that when a brand wishes to be seen and heard by a large section of society, its presence in media and entertainment—principally in the form of ads—is paid for by that brand. The practice continues to this day.

While paid media is still a large chunk of all brand media, with digital now taking a 20 per cent share of the pie, today's brands can earn significant amounts of media coverage by engaging in popular culture and through having a point of view on social themes. Great branded content becomes material customers want to share with friends and family. Brands also share platforms with other brands and with like-minded celebrities and public figures to get additional coverage in the media.

While media remains a largely expense-driven activity, a genuine public image can get a brand a much louder bang for its buck through earned and shared media.

Points 1–8 of the Visible DNA contribute to the customer experience, product interface and storytelling sides of the Brand Octagon.

* * *

Are there any Indian brands that are truly authentic or at least more down the road to being so? I can think of three: Nappa Dori, Nimba and IndiGo.

Nappa Dori

Nappa Dori is a relatively new (2010) handcrafted leather accessories brand. The name translates as 'leather and thread'. They offer genuine leather products handcrafted by traditional artisans, marrying Indian images with modern designs.

The core of any brand answers these three questions: Why are you here? What do you do? How do you do it?

Why does Nappa Dori exist? To imbue contemporary interpretations in design, material and craftsmanship with a quintessentially Indian sensibility.

What do they do? They make leather accessories and luggage, handcrafted by traditional artisans.

How do they do it? Through a unique mix of design and craftsmanship that infuses the nostalgia and mysticism of Indian culture into accessories and luggage that appear sophisticated and subtly elegant.

The performance of Nappa Dori laptop cases, travel bags, card cases, wallets and so on is beyond reproach. They handle everyday use very well, without showing any signs of damage or wear. The designs, which use beautifully shot images of India, mark their customers out as people with good taste.

The product interface is easy, enjoyable and very satisfactory. And because not too many people own Nappa Dori products, there's a pleasurable feeling of exclusivity connected to the brand. The pricing is just expensive enough for you to know that you're getting something special, and yet not so expensive that you question the value or start to compare the brand with a major fashion label. The service is great, whether at one of their stores, online or at Café Dori. At the Nappa Dori stores, the staff leave you to browse at your own pace and are on hand to guide or assist when you need them.

Nappa Dori's corporate social responsibility ('Impact on Planet') has them contributing a portion of their profits to Harmony House, a day shelter that provides free food, accommodation, clothing, education and medical care to destitute children. Their website and emails to customers and subscribers on their mailing list—the storytelling side of their Brand Octagon—allow their products to speak for themselves through well-laid-out and beautifully photographed compositions.

The overall customer experience: very satisfying.

Marks out of ten for brand authenticity: seven. (Had they been doing more to offset the toxic environmental impact of the leather industry, I'd have given them a higher score.)

Nimba

Nimba Nature Cure is a naturopathy and wellness retreat about an hour's drive from Ahmedabad on the highway to Mehsana in Gujarat. It occupies 14 acres of a 40-acre plot and offers residential treatment for a range of respiratory, gastrointestinal, musculoskeletal, endocrine and lifestyle diseases. The method is essentially following a customized plan for each visitor that includes diet, Ayurvedic treatments, yoga, cardio exercise, physiotherapy, hydrotherapy and music therapy.

The campus—including its gardens, treatment areas, residences, dining hall, yoga pavilion, swimming pool—has been built with exemplary attention to detail. At dawn and sunset, concealed speakers all around the campus softly play the sound of Aum. The quality of medical advice and treatment is impeccable. The food, intentionally bland for obvious reasons, is easily more than palatable. And yet, Nimba is far from being the most expensive place you could go to for a naturopathy cure in India.

What sets Nimba truly apart is its genuineness. The medical team, the therapists, the housekeepers, the catering staff, even the gardeners and security team seem genuinely keen to ensure that the visitor is comfortable, happy and gets better from whichever problem they have come to treat. The concern is real, the smiles are real and their delight in seeing a visitor's progress is real.

Marks out of ten for brand authenticity: eight. (Had they been doing more to reduce their heavy use of water, unavoidable in their treatments, I'd have given them a higher score.)

IndiGo

IndiGo is a genuine Indian success story which has transformed air travel in India.

In thirteen years of operation, IndiGo has grown its fleet from one aircraft to 256 and has become India's largest passenger airline, even as its competitors have come and gone. IndiGo primarily operates in India's domestic air travel market, offering low fares, promising on-time arrivals and departures, and delivering a hassle-free experience. Today, they are India's most preferred airline.

IndiGo constantly augments its engagement with passengers to enhance their travel experience. At IndiGo, low fares come with high quality. The courtesy they extend to passengers comes from their work culture. A highly engaged and motivated workforce leads to better customer service. IndiGo's state-of-the-art aviation training facility is considered to be one of the best in India, and they are among the best organizations to work for in the country. Their corporate social responsibility initiative, IndiGoReach, focuses on three broad themes: children and education, women's empowerment and environment.

Alongside all these admirable achievements, two characteristics that mark IndiGo as a truly authentic brand are:

1. The absence of arrogance or smugness on account of success. IndiGo's staff continues to be humble and service-minded. The captains and in-flight crew leaders unfailingly thank passengers on board for flying with IndiGo. The ground staff announce flight information and boarding sequences professionally and with service in mind.

2. IndiGo stopped advertising some years ago. They don't need to. When they did, it was delightful. Their current storytelling methodology—involving primarily their in-flight magazine, emails or labels on food containers— is interesting, charismatic and uses language that reflects IndiGo's quirky personality.

Marks out of ten for brand authenticity: nine. (Had they done something to sort out the long and tedious baggage-drop and check-in queues at their airport counters, I'd have given them a higher score.)

Section 3

How to Go to Market

VII

How to Talk to People

Nugget 7: Creating Powerful Brand Content

'*The art of communication is the language of leadership.*'

—James Humes

Communicating successfully with people who want to hear you is hard, and it is even harder to communicate with people who don't want to listen to you. Creating standout brand content that speaks to people who want to listen—and to people who don't—has never been a bigger challenge than it is in the present day. Budgets are never infinite. Communicating powerfully and efficiently to get the largest possible bang for one's marketing buck is as much a need today as it was when marketing began.

There is so much to learn from John Wanamaker (1838–1922), the legendary American entrepreneur and pioneer of many of the practices of marketing that are in use today. In 1861, he started Oak Hall, a men's and boys' clothing shop, which could be thought of as the prototype of the modern-day department store. Wanamaker's attention to customer service saw the store flourish. Although many merchants at the time scoffed at the idea of a 'sale', Wanamaker ran special sales at Oak Hall for their customers.

In 1868, Wanamaker opened a second store in Philadelphia. He called this new store John Wanamaker & Co. After the store opened, Wanamaker published the first-ever copyrighted advertisement by a retailer. A few years later, in 1875, on the back of the success of his new business, he bought the former Pennsylvania Railroad depot at Thirteenth and Market Streets in Philadelphia to open another store called the Grand Depot.

Wanamaker is credited with many of marketing's 'firsts'. His store was the forerunner to the one-stop shopping centre of the future, and it was the first such facility to expand its product line to sell women's items and dry goods as well. He was the first to set up a restaurant in a general store, the first to send a team overseas (in 1876) to study retail practices in foreign markets, the first to use electric lighting in a store and the first to use unique marketing tactics like 'white sales' (offering discounted prices on all white-coloured products in his store).

In 1879, Wanamaker became the first merchant in America to bring out full-page newspaper advertisements. He rented horse-drawn carriages draped with advertisements and hired 'sandwich men' who carried advertising signs of his stores and walked around Philadelphia.[1]

---

[1] Source: https://pabook.libraries.psu.edu/literary-cultural-heritage-map-pa/bios/Wanamaker__John

John Wanamaker once said, 'Half the money I spend on advertising is wasted. The trouble is I don't know which half.' To be sure, its echoes have travelled over time and are still heard in today's marketing world. The idea that marketing communication has large inefficiencies has been with us for over a century. The practice of brand communication aims to reduce, if not eliminate, these inefficiencies.

Two basic routes exist to reduce communication inefficiencies. One, make the message sharper. Two, make the media buying better. A metaphor for this—probably almost as old as Wanamaker's statement—is the way a nail and hammer function. The nail is the message; the hammer is the media spend. The sharper the nail (the better the creativity), the smaller the size of the hammer required to drive it into a wall. Conversely, the blunter the nail, the larger the hammer required.

The brand communication industry has continuously grown in expertise over the decades as various practitioners took individual approaches to creating sharper nails and smaller hammers.

David Ogilvy (1911–99) was a British advertising tycoon, founder of Ogilvy & Mather and popularly known as the 'Father of Advertising'. (I worked at Ogilvy and Mather India from 1986–93 and had the unmatched pleasure of meeting David twice. I learnt so much from him, even in those brief meetings.) Trained at the Gallup research organization, he attributed the success of his campaigns to meticulous research into consumer habits. ('Don't count the people you reach; reach the people who count,' as he once said.) Ogilvy & Mather was founded on David Ogilvy's principles, one of them being that the function of advertising is to sell. ('If it doesn't sell, it isn't creative.') He disliked advertisements that had loud, patronizing voices and believed that a customer should be treated as an intelligent person. ('The customer is not a moron; she is your wife.')

Ogilvy was one of the early practitioners whose ideas contributed towards making the advertising industry more creative than ever. There were many others. William Bernbach (1911–82), co-founder of the agency Doyle Dane Bernbach, among them. Bernbach agreed with Ogilvy that 'the purpose of advertising is to sell'. He also agreed with Ogilvy about the role of information: 'The most powerful element in advertising is the truth.' Unlike Ogilvy, however, Bernbach did not set much store by research: 'We are so busy measuring public opinion that we forget we can mold it. We are so busy listening to statistics we forget we can create them.' About the essence of advertising, Bernbach felt, 'Advertising is fundamentally persuasion, and persuasion happens to be not a science, but an art.'

The start given by industry legends like Ogilvy, Bernbach, Rosser Reeves, Leo Burnett and many others inspired successive generations of creative craftsmen, like John Hegarty of Bartle Bogle Hegarty, and Lee Clow of TBWA\Chiat\Day.

The nails kept getting sharper.

On the hammer side, too, much was happening. While message development focused on the one person the brand wanted to talk to, the point of placing ads in media was to reach as many people as possible, with as small a spend as possible. Before the printing press, drummers—the original salesmen—travelled far and wide and 'drummed up' business. With the advent of the printing press, handbills and newspapers became the preferred mediums. Radio did not just make it possible to carry an audio message for the brand but also ushered in the idea of programme sponsorships. 'This programme is brought to you by . . .' is a convention that continues to this day. Cinemas became widespread, running commercials prior to the main feature. Television—along with radio—further popularized the concept of entertainment sponsored by brands, with its 'soap operas', 'soaps' for short, named so because their early sponsors were soap manufacturers. Audiences became familiar with, and often deeply involved in, television or radio drama serials dealing typically with the daily events in the lives of the same group of characters. Interestingly, audiences of that time welcomed radio and TV commercials from brands, unlike the present-day ad-averse audiences. Ads were a means to know what was available to them. And so, another convention was born, which continues to this day: the 'price' of watching broadcast entertainment was to have it interrupted at regular intervals by commercials from brand sponsors.

Connected to the growth of the media and entertainment industries is the growth of the audience measurement industry. In the days of the newspaper's ascendancy, the National Readership Survey's data in this regard was paramount. Later, as the measurement of cinema, radio and TV audiences began, the statistical process increased in sophistication and the numbers arrived faster at the desks of media planners so they could make real-time decisions. These researches allowed media planners to make better deals with media owners, bringing greater efficiency to a brand's media spends.

So the hammer was getting better as well.

The creative and media sides of brand communication are obviously complementary, and yet so different in approach and personality. If message developers (creatives) see their work as an art, message placers (media folk) see their work as a science. If people in the creative department seem bohemian, those in media planning appear almost boring and conventional. If message is about persuasion, media is about presence. If creative is about reducing audiences to that one person you can talk to, media is about expanding the numbers to as many people the brand can reach. This interplay between the two sides of brand communication is eternal.

Global brand communication blueprints

By the early 1990s, many brands had gone global. The direct control the 'head office', typically in a Western city, could exert on a brand's marketing decisions diminished with globalization. The need to bring common, worldwide disciplines to brand communication was born. Large multinationals, Unilever and Procter & Gamble among them, created exportable 'templates' for brand communication. These templates distilled the multinational's brand communication learning into principles, processes and practices that could travel with their brands all over the world. The goal was to fuse the art and science of brand communication into a single blueprint.

In the mid-1990s, Unilever trained its brand people, and their partner agencies, all over the world in a method they called Advanced Brand Communication (ABC). The initialism ABC had a second meaning as well: attention, branding, communication. Any piece of communication a brand put out needed to get attention, be recognized for the brand it came from and deliver its message. As advertising agency Lowe & Partners' regional account director on Unilever for Middle East and North Africa at that time, I had the privilege to be appointed as one of Unilever's original ambassadors who delivered the ABC training. My role was to partner with a client in delivering the training to the Middle East and North Africa region. This gave me an intimate understanding of ABC, in both the meanings of the initialism.

The first aim of any piece of communication is to get *attention*. Without attention, no information transfer can take place.

The second is to *brand* it strongly, so that the viewer knows who it's from.

The third is to deliver the message. In other words, to *communicate*.

Obviously, ABC did not suggest that this was a sequence to be followed. The A, B and C were to be harmoniously intertwined and achieve all three aims.

Unilever's ABC—attention, branding, communication—is a handy 'formula' for creating content to this day. Although not explicitly stated in the initialism, a central idea of ABC is that communication should make an impact on its audience, creating a desired attitude, belief or action. I am taking the liberty to make these two points explicit, by adding to Unilever's original ABC a fourth and a fifth letter. D for the audiences *decoding* the communication in a personally relevant way; and E for *engagement*, which I use as a catch-all for attitudes, beliefs and actions.

My modified formula for brand communication—with sincere gratitude and respect to Unilever for the original—is ABCDE.

A – Attention
B – Branding
C – Communication
D – Decoding
E – Engagement

Using ABCDE as a guideline, marketers can address the point James Humes makes in the quotation that opens this chapter. They can use great communication as an instrument for brand and business leadership. A measurement-inclined marketer, a 'science' marketer if you like, can use research to check success at every level—attention (did you notice it?); branding (who was it from?), communication (what did it say?); decoding (what does that mean for you?); engagement (what does that make you feel and do?). The 'art' marketer can use it as a whetstone for developing sharp communication skills.

The arrival of the Internet

In the 1990s, technology brought the convergence of telephony, computing, information and entertainment, and soon the term 'digital revolution' could be heard everywhere. From a brand marketing point of view, the Internet really arrived in the 2000s. Marketing on the Internet started to gain momentum in India from the 2010s. It took time for marketers to get to grips with digital, or online as it is interchangeably called, and the learning process is still very much on. By contrast, the depth of understanding of offline, the traditional methods of marketing communication, is vast and has matured over the last century.

Digital's share of total communication spend has grown to 20 per cent over the last two decades as marketers have understood it better. But digital's gain has been the traditional media's loss, impacting newspapers and magazines as well as TV and radio.

When the Internet first arrived, whatever marketing activity it hosted was without much clarity or purpose. Marketers who were early users of the Internet were not unlike wildcatters tramping across vast expanses of uncharted territory, randomly digging holes to see if they could strike oil. They sponsored websites, put out banner ads, worked on brand apps, tried to be interesting on Facebook and took up a range of other experiments. Many of these failed of course, but that is part and parcel of experimentation.

Today, twenty years on, a new clarity has emerged. What has changed? Information is digital. Entertainment is digital. Utilities are digital. Shopping is digital. Social media has been born.

The impact of digital on traditional businesses is well-documented. Many long-standing brands went into terminal decline, while others are a shadow of their former selves.

The shift of marcom spends to digital platforms has made many news and entertainment brands financially unviable. Today, new brands like Google and Facebook attract huge shares of marcom spends, as do a range of other digital channels.

The Internet is also responsible for four other profound changes which make a significant impact on the brand communication ecosystem.

First, the centre of gravity of customer attention is shifting away from TV and print to the Internet. When it comes to looking up or researching anything, the Internet is pretty much the first door to knock. If print, radio and TV were the leading mass unifiers in the past century, the Internet is the mass unifier of the present and the future.

Second, the long-accepted convention of advertising being an interloper in the information and entertainment landscape has been disrupted. More and more customers, especially younger ones, whom brands could previously reach through ads, now subscribe to ad-free (or ad-skip) music, video and news services. Research shows urban Indians between the ages of twenty-two and thirty-seven spend around 69 per cent of their video time on YouTube, 29 per cent on Amazon Prime Video, 20 per cent on Google Play, 18 per cent on Netflix and 15 per cent on Voot.[2] And these numbers—with new streaming brands and more India-targeted original programming—will rise year on year.

Third, the screen time on all devices is increasing. According to an eMarketer.com survey published in

---

[2]   Source: https://www.emarketer.com/chart/226631/which-platforms-do-millennials-urban-india-use-consume-digital-video-content-regularly-of-respondents-july-2018

July 2019, the average time India spent on all screens in 2017 was 4.13 hours, of which TV constituted 59.5 per cent and digital (smartphone, feature phone, tablet and desktop) 27.7 per cent. In 2019 those numbers stood at 4.59 hours in total, 58.7 per cent for TV and 29.9 per cent for digital. The estimate for 2021 is 5.24 hours, with TV at 57.5 per cent and digital at 31.6 per cent.[3]

Within digital, the share of smartphones will rise by 6 per cent by 2021. These numbers still show a sizeable viewership for TV, because in India we still have vast numbers watching TV in small towns and rural areas. The penetration of smartphones among women, who are a huge part of India's TV audiences, is much lower than among men, especially in small towns. The digital share in big cities and among the young demographic in small towns is much higher.

Fourth, if in the past, an ad on TV had to essentially compete with the channel's programming to stand out and be noticed, today the battle for attention is fought against everything a customer can access through any medium or platform they choose. The sensory threshold for making an impact is at an all-time high. Communication which is just average in terms of quality is unlikely to get attention, let alone deliver its message. According to Digitalinformationworld. com, the average human attention span was 8.25 seconds in 2015, down from twelve seconds in 2000.[4] That's less than

---

[3]   Source: https://www.emarketer.com/content/india-time-spent-with-media-2019

[4]   'The Human Attention Span', DigitalInformationWorld.com, 10 September 2018, https://www.digitalinformationworld.com/2018/09/the-human-attention-span-infographic.html

a goldfish's attention span, estimated at nine seconds. And if it was 8.25 seconds in 2015, what would it be in 2020 and beyond?

Strategy framework for brand communication

Taking all this into account, a strategy fit for the present times should have five components:

1. Communicate across the entire customer journey
2. Make a comprehensive broadcast and narrowcast plan
3. Deploy the entire Brand Octagon in communication
4. Create a pipeline for superlative branded content
5. Measure performance and be nimble to change

1. Communicate across the entire customer journey

Many Indian brands focus communication on a single aspect, or at best on a few aspects related to a central concern: acquiring customers. A reason for this is that companies are split into departments. Marketing's job is often only to bring customers through the door; meeting their needs might fall into the hands of operations, managing their complaints in the hands of customer service and so on. Each department will have a head and its own people, as well as its own objectives and performance measures, and thus silos are created. While everyone is working for the success of the brand and company, common measurements of customer satisfaction elude the team, and with it a comprehensive communication plan across the entire customer journey.

I go into more details of my model of the customer-brand relationship journey in Chapter 9. But let me briefly touch upon the main aspects here from purely a communication point of view.

Any customer-brand relationship journey has four elements: discovery, companionship, exclusivity and belonging. During *discovery*, a customer is finding out about you, a brand she doesn't know or knows only a little. She might be exploring a curiosity about a new category, one she hasn't participated in before, through you. In *companionship*, a customer is spending time with your brand as she expands her research, but she is also spending time with other brands. She is making comparisons, asking for advice and looking at reviews by previous users. In *exclusivity*, she is making a choice in favour of your brand. This might seem like a moment of triumph for the brand, a completion of the acquisition, but in actual fact this is where the hard work begins. Because when a customer chooses your brand, *she lays all her expectations from the category at your brand's door.* Your onboarding has to be great, as well as your subsequent actions. Most important, your brand must now meet pretty much all her expectations from the category, even those that might not be among the strengths of your brand. Finally there's *belonging*, where the customer is so happy and fulfilled by your brand that she repeats her business with you or makes your brand a regular part of her customer journey.

Brand communication for each of these stages is different. What a brand must say and do during the discovery stage is very different from what it must say and do during the companionship, exclusivity or belonging stages.

Discovery will take you into online search engine optimization and search engine marketing (SEO and SEM), along with perhaps a TV ad, a few pay-per-click ads and so on. Companionship will take you into comparison sites, influencer recommendations, customer reviews. Exclusivity will take you into emails, phone calls and complaint management. Belonging could take you into special offers and celebratory discounts.

If a brand takes a holistic view of the customer-brand relationship journey, great things will come to it. If it takes a siloed view, the number of not-so-happy customers is likely to be high.

2. Make a comprehensive broadcast and narrowcast plan

I am firmly of the view that it is high time marcom moved away from the legacy pillars of communication strategy. Typically, a brand communication plan is structured as, 'We will do X on TV, Y in print, Z in digital and so on.' Sometimes the individual elements join up well; often they don't. A media-led marcom strategy is unhelpful in today's times.

The right pillars for marcom strategy in today's times are two: broadcast and narrowcast.

The broadcast pillar has simple messages, executed in video or as ads in newspapers and retail, pitched at a wide spectrum of customers, offering one common-interest idea of the brand. Broadcast might be delivered on TV, on YouTube, in an online newspaper, in a Facebook feed or as a link sent by email. The medium isn't the main thing here;

the main thing is that a simple message is sent to many and presents only a single broad-interest idea about the brand. It might be about the brand's performance or about the brand's work on reducing its environmental impact or indeed about something else. Broadcast may not ask for any immediate response from the customer, other than they watch, listen to and decode the message. And hopefully, it would permanently attach this piece of information to their thoughts about the brand.

The narrowcast pillar has more layered communication and could be two-way, inviting a dialogue or action. It is targeted to a single customer or to a small group joined by a common perspective or interest. How was your last flight with us? How was your stay at our hotel? Would you like to track your package? May we request you to post your review on such-and-such a site? May we call you with a special offer? Narrowcast is between the brand and the individual customer. It allows the brand to listen, as well as to speak, and deal with issues in a more personalized manner.

The narrowcast pillar also allows a brand to harness the power of influencers and of the undecided neutrals. The personality of a particular influencer might not appeal to an entire brand user base, but it might have disproportionate influence with a specific subset of customers. Narrowcast allows a brand to test an offer and launch a small-volume product aimed at this subset. Narrowcast also gives a brand an avenue to direct specific communication at undecided customers, those who might not have made up their minds yet on which brand to purchase.

If brands marry broadcast and narrowcast with the customer relationship journey I mentioned earlier, a new precision in the communication plan will start to emerge almost by itself.

3.   Deploy the entire Brand Octagon in communication

Some brands choose to only speak about their performance. 'We wash whiter.' 'We go farther per litre of fuel.' 'Our paints withstand the harshest elements.'

That's like a superhero using just one of his eight superpowers.

Brands can draw great power from each side of the Brand Octagon. Not everyone would be interested in all eight sides, but there still might be some—likely many—willing to utilize the entire Octagon.

A cosmetics brand's 'We do not test on animals' stand might not make it into broadcast communication, but consigning it to a small line on the back label would be a mistake. Why not unleash the power of this message in suitable media? Make it a pre-roll on animal care videos on YouTube? Drop it on to pet sites?

Apart from the eight sides of the Brand Octagon, the core has great power too. Customers are interested in asking a brand: Why are you here? What do you do? How do you do it? A founder's speech to the company staff about these points, made available through a blog that can be accessed on Facebook, might be a great way to get these points out. And at a low cost too.

Different people have different takes on your brand. They assess your brand through different lenses based on what they feel is important. A brand holds within its Octagon the power to engage most points of customer interest. So deploy the entire Octagon.

If brands marry the Brand Octagon with broadcast, narrowcast and the customer relationship journey, a beautiful fit between brand advantages and audience interests will be immediately visible along with pointers on when, where and how to communicate.

4.   Create a pipeline for superlative branded content

Branded content is about great storytelling. You need to tell your brand's stories well. And you need to have lots of stories to tell. Brands have to be like Shahrazad, (the customer being Shahryar), in the fabled Middle Eastern folk tales *The Thousand and One Nights*.

These stories—a large collection of tales about adventure, romance, magic and fantasy—are held together by a single overarching narrative. This narrative concerns King Shahryar, who has killed his wife after learning of her infidelity. He has also killed all her lovers. Driven to an extreme by his resentment, he remarries and kills a new wife every day. The elder of his vizier's two daughters, Shahrazad, having devised a scheme to save herself and others, marries the king. Each evening, Shahrazad tells Shahryar a story, but she leaves it incomplete and promises to narrate the rest of it the following night. Eager to hear the end every time, the king keeps postponing Shahrazad's execution, eventually sparing her life.

A good parallel: brands and customers, like Shahrazad and Shahryar.

Brands need to continually tell customers fascinating stories, like Shahrazad does to Shahryar, to keep them engaged and committed. Unlike The Thousand and One Nights *though, brand stories need to be unfailingly authentic and rooted in brand truth.*

How does a brand tell great stories?

All great stories essentially follow a simple formula, nuances and expressions of which are seen across genres in books, films, television and web shows. Whether romantic comedy or action film, they have a common set of ingredients:

A hero: an ordinary person, unaware of a hidden ability or a higher calling.

A call to action: a person or problem threatens something or someone valuable to her.

She shies away from the problem, or perhaps tries to deal with it, but meets with failure.

A mentor arrives unbidden, or she goes in search of one.

A period of preparation: she may recruit a team from fellow trainees.

A day arrives when she re-confronts the problem, or an embodiment of the main threat.

Success emboldens her and her team.

They take on the main person or problem.

A battle ensues.

Just when all seems lost, the hero finds a hidden reserve that brings victory.

The good guys celebrate.

Our hero returns to a simple life, but with an awareness of a higher ability and calling.

Strange though it may sound, most brand stories mirror this eternal structure. They might not do so at every step, but the parallels hold at many if not most steps.

A teenage girl finds a zit on her face a week before prom night. What is she to do? What will her date think? She wonders whether she should go to the prom. A friend recommends a brand of anti-acne cream. She uses it and the zit is gone in just three days. She looks radiant. She goes to the prom. They have a marvellous time. The evening was perfect, thanks to that brand of anti-acne cream.

A brand realizes that there's too much plastic polluting the planet and that the brand itself is responsible for at least some of it. The brand wants to change that. It takes on a mission: less or no plastic in packaging. It reinvents itself and goes plastic-free. It is now a brand that's better for the planet.

See the parallels? I am not suggesting that every story has to be told strictly in this manner. The story should be told through the brand's personality and in the brand's voice. All I am saying is great storytelling has a narrative structure that brands can use.

How does a brand create a pipeline of great stories?

In a TV show or movie, it's the writing—sometimes by one writer but more often by a group of writers—that creates magic on the screen. Writers dedicate themselves to creating the narrative arc of a single character of a TV show. They work with producers, directors and technicians. They have the skills and talent to write the content according to the requirements of the characters and the story. But the rest of the team takes over when the content is in the production, release and post-analysis stages. Some call this a 'content factory'.

That's what brands need today. Unlike what happens in the entertainment sector, which allows for a group to be assembled for the period of the production exclusively focused on the narrative needs of a single story, marketers have to deal with small bundles of talent scattered across many associates. A team in the advertising agency 'gets' the brand, a digital media buyer in another agency 'gets' the brand and so on. In other words, marketers have to play a continuous talent-aggregation role in the interest of their brand narratives.

In general, the need for newer and better brand stories is as acute as for the next episode or next season of a successful serial.

In order to build a content pipeline, marketers must demand and receive the best talent across the agencies they use. They should assemble them as a team to work seamlessly together, ignoring the company names on their business cards. They are no longer members of their companies; they are on the brand team. The marketer must provide this team with a steady supply of news from all sides of the Brand Octagon, as well as reports about improvements, innovations, successes, new initiatives, new products. The glue that binds the team and the work is the brand.

5. Measure performance and be nimble to change

A vital part of communication is listening. Learning to listen, understanding what is being said, using what has been heard. And measurement is an organized, structured form of listening. Measurement is important because you can't change what you can't measure.

Today, so much of marketing—pretty much all of it— can be measured. So measure everything. But don't become a slave to numbers, of course. Don't let the numbers lead you; let them guide you. Let both David Ogilvy and Bill Bernbach be your guides: don't get so busy measuring public opinion that you forget to mould it; don't get so busy listening to statistics that you forget to create them. Practise both the science and the art of marketing. Trust your intellect and your intuition.

And be open and quick to change. Keep experimenting when you fail. Keep experimenting even when you succeed. Remain open to customer changes and movements. That's the way to keep your brand abreast of culture, and perhaps even a little ahead of it.

VIII

How to Create Strong Connections

Nugget 8: A Model for 'Differentiated Relevance'

'My major ambition is just to stay relevant . . .'

—James Corden, British actor and comedian[1]

British author Sir Arthur Conan Doyle's fictional consulting detective Sherlock Holmes first appeared in print in the 1887 novel *A Study in Scarlet*. The first complete series of Sherlock Holmes short stories appeared in 1891, and many more were published until 1927. At the final count, Doyle had written four Holmes novels and fifty-six short stories. Most of the stories are told through the eyes of Holmes's faithful friend and flatmate, Dr Watson, who assists Holmes and is the chronicler of their cases. Dr Watson also helps in another way: he is the always staunch, frequently admiring but

---

[1] Lisa Campbell, 'James Corden: "My Major Ambition Is Just to Stay Relevant, to Be in the Conversation"', *Guardian*, 17 July 2016, https://www.theguardian. com/media/2016/jul/17/james-corden-michelle-obama-carpool-karaoke

perpetually puzzled sideman to whom Holmes must explain his deductions (for the benefit of the reader). Characterized by a cold, logical, unromantic mind and using methods such as minute physical examination of crime scenes and forensic science, the character of Holmes (and Watson) rapidly gained popularity not just in the England of that time but all over the world, and the character is as popular today. Most of the Holmes stories, set between about 1880 and 1914, begin at the flat Holmes and Watson share, and use as an office: 221B Baker Street, a fictional address whose real-world near equivalent in London is a tourist attraction.

There have been many big- and small-screen productions of the Sherlock Holmes stories. Some adaptations have looked at Holmes as a child, while others have transplanted him from London to New York, turning Watson into a woman along the way. Two recent Guy Ritchie films have a very 'physical' Holmes, as opposed to the intellectual one fans are used to, fighting foes old and new (including supernatural ones), helped in great measure by a feisty and pugilistic Watson, a very different characterization from the unimaginative stolidity of the Watson of the original stories. That said, the most widely appreciated Holmes adaptations are made for television: the Peter Cushing and Nigel Stock series from 1964–68; the Jeremy Brett and Edward Hardwicke series from 1984–94; and the 2010 reboot, starring Benedict Cumberbatch and Martin Freeman, which relocate the duo and their most popular adventures to modern times, where they solve present-day crimes using modern methods and technology.

What is fascinating about these cinematic interpretations is the manner in which successive generations of viewers have enthusiastically embraced Holmes, Watson and their stories. What has made this possible? The writers have, by finding brilliant new ways to update the characters and plots. Every new production refreshes the appeal of Holmes and Watson, connecting them to a new generation, creating new fans. Purists might argue that each new production takes the characters further away from the original, but few will dispute that if Sherlock Holmes is holding his own today, despite the onslaught of the *Avengers*, *Game of Thrones* and *Fast & Furious* franchises, it is due to the modern twist given to his Victorian appeal.

But what is perhaps the greatest tribute to Holmes, or indeed to any brand, takes us back to the original books. Fearing (wrongly) that the public would soon tire of Holmes, and wanting to do away with him before this happened, Conan Doyle had Holmes fatally plunge over the Reichenbach Falls, locked in combat with his arch-enemy Professor Moriarty, in the story 'The Final Problem'. The storm of protest this generated from loyal fans was so loud and incessant that it forced Conan Doyle to bring Holmes back to life and continue his adventures in subsequent novels and stories.

What wouldn't any brand give to have such a passionate following that its users demand its continuance, even if its creators want to put it to rest!

Sherlock Holmes is a terrific example of a brand that has found ways to connect with customers not just for a short time but for over a century. This is vital because the graveyard of marketing is crammed with the tombstones of many once-great brands, such as Kodak, Trans World

Airlines, HMV, Nokia, Chiclets and Blockbuster Video, which failed to connect to new audiences. Closer to home, Forhan's, Anacin, Hindustan Motors' Ambassador, Premier Padmini and Luna have all failed the test of time.

On the other hand, there are brands that have, like Sherlock Holmes, prospered for decades, even centuries. Shell, Walmart, Axe, Gillette, Head & Shoulders and Microsoft continue to flourish, refreshing and rejuvenating themselves, finding ways past difficulties, using adversity to make themselves stronger, always making new brand-consumer connections. Reliance, Tata and a host of Indian brands have also stood the test of time, going from strength to strength.

What makes the difference between flourishing and perishing?

In one word, *connection*. Staying connected to customers, year after year, decade after decade, generation after generation. Adapting to changes in consumer interests and lifestyles, creating new meanings and roles for the brand despite the changes having to do with where people live, how they live, with whom they live and what attitudes and expectations they have.

So, not a static, one-time or short-term connection that is 'up like a rocket and down like a stick', but instead a dynamic, adaptive and evolutionary connection that keeps the brand relevant not for one or a few generations of consumers, but for endless successive generations.

The key question, of course, is how. How does one forge, protect and grow brand connections?

Let me give you a simple formula to think of this.

Formula for brand connection

CONTACT + INFORMATION = KNOWLEDGE

KNOWLEDGE + RELEVANCE = ENGAGEMENT

ENGAGEMENT = DIFFERENTIATION = PREFERENCE

PREFERENCE + ESTEEM = DESIRE

DESIRE + PRICING = DEMAND

Let's now unpack this formula.

The first construct is *knowledge*, which results from an interaction between *contact* and *information.*

When it comes to *contact*, two obvious questions arise. First, contact with whom? Second: Where, and to what end?

Looking at the first question, obviously a well-defined and well-understood audience is central to the idea of contact. In today's times, an audience is not a homogeneous group of single-identity customers (see Chapter 1 of this book). Even within a specified target audience, a brand appeals to a number of ages, income segments and geographic locations. More importantly, customers split into multiple-identity subsets, based on their needs, motivations and action orientations (Chapters 2 and 3).

A brand's audience extends beyond customers to purchasers, influencers, references, advisers, showrooms, distributors, flagship stores, brick-and-mortar retailers, online retailers, delivery fulfillers, competitors, suppliers,

government regulators, NGOs, CSR beneficiaries and
so on. Asian Paints would list homeowners, architects,
painting contractors, their flagship paint studios and paint
dealers among their audiences. Kia Motors would make
car comparison sites a vital addition to its audience list.
Publishers would have literary reviewers on their lists;
restaurants would have food critics; baby care brands would
have birthing-room nurses; and hotels would have travel
aggregators.

All brands know a range of audiences can influence
their success. But few have the desire, ability or effectiveness
to holistically reach out to them. Sometimes one section of
the audience gets a disproportionate preference, resulting
in a prejudice against others or even in a key audience being
ignored to the detriment of the brand. It is true that limited
marketing budgets impose constraints, but choices made at
the cost of holistic marketing prove expensive in the long run.

New language to describe customer groups—such
as tribes and cohorts—promise much, because they
signal superior segmentation criteria to replace the dusty
descriptors still in widespread use in India today. They point
to customer groups bound by an attitudinal, behavioural and
emotional glue much more profound than the accidents of
age, gender and location. A tribe or cohort is alike in world
view, purpose, aesthetic preferences and tastes—all of which
are extremely valuable to marketers. They are also more
similar than different in behaviour. Behavioural analysis
has become even more valuable in recent times, emerging
as it has as one of the most potent of the new criteria for
predicting business outcomes.

A podcast recorded by the British magazine *Marketing Week* explores how marketers in the UK are using new criteria to segment and target audiences.[2] A survey they conducted revealed that 91 per cent of marketers felt 'behaviour' was the most useful segmentation criterion. 'Age' dropped to a low seventh in its usefulness. Only 25 per cent of the sample felt 'social class' was useful. Out of the sample interviewed, 93 per cent felt labels like 'millennials', 'Gen Z' and 'Gen X' were new stereotypes of little, if any, use. Understanding people through their needs, interests and motivations trumped recognizing them in accordance with whichever age bracket they fell in. The dominant majority felt that a multi-criteria, multilayered approach to describing and targeting audiences was the most useful. The finance portal MoneySuperMarket. com is known for this. Their hybrid method of targeting audiences takes multilayering to a high level, combining life stage, demographics, customer needs, attitudes and behaviours with 700 data points.

Significantly, the UK marketers interviewed in the podcast said that the media is lagging behind in the field of marketing and must catch up. This relates to the point I made earlier in this book, that *single-identity customers are a media convenience*, far from an adequate or accurate depiction of the people we market to.

Which makes for a nice segue into the second question about *contact*: Where, and with what purpose?

---

[2] 'The New Rules of Segmentation: Demographics in Decline and Rethinking Tired Stereotypes', *Marketing Week*, 24 April 2019, https://www.marketingweek. com/demographics-over-50s-market-podcast/

As in the UK, India's marketers are handicapped by the constraints of media. This is as true of online marketing as it is of offline. Whether television and print or programmatic buying, media is essentially sold by numbers, in big blocks, not unlike farm produce at a commodities exchange. Marketers buy demographically defined inventory, not value-added targeting. This sometimes leads to the cynical speculation that the media industry is invested in keeping media buying in present-day stasis, on account of not having found a way to navigate past their time-honoured markers of reach and impressions. Offline media only offers ad placement, with no commitments on performance. Online media is also largely sold in a similar fashion, with the addition of CTR (click-through rate) as a measure of performance. Significantly, India's average CTR is 2 per cent, suggesting that 98 per cent of online media buying is a waste—a statistic that offline media shares.

It is clear that the current media buying practices do not help in providing value-added answers to 'Where, and with what purpose?' (In the next chapter, I share two models that will help answer this.)

The only brands that get past media's 'Where, and with what purpose' shortcomings are those with a direct digital access to their customers, such as Amazon, Flipkart, Spotify, IndiGo and Booking.com. They have direct access to consumer behaviour and can achieve the multi-criteria, multilayered targeting mentioned earlier. They can use permission marketing, asking for and receiving customers' consent to send messages to their phones and inboxes.

The second aspect of *knowledge* is *information*.

Most brands prefer managing information on their own terms. They would ideally like to exclusively control what is said about their brand, when it is said, how often, by whom and to whom. In the more distant yesteryear, this was possible: brands ran TV ads or print campaigns, giving the customer a phone number or postal address for inquiries and complaints. The brand controlled what their customers saw. Any adverse feedback and complaints were handled discreetly, outside the public eye. More recently, brands began providing email ids, toll-free helplines and service phone calls for feedback. When websites extended the reach of brand-generated communication, information about the brand still largely remained in the brand owner's control. Less flattering feedback was controllable; its visibility could be contained to an acceptable percentage. Today, with an explosion in users and of self-publishing platforms provided by social media, it is a whole different matter. Brand information is no longer in the brand's exclusive control. On Facebook and Twitter, consumers challenge a brand's claims, quality, service and reputation, and air grievances for all to see. Consumers are frequently harsh and judgemental, shaming brands into defensive positions and after-the-fact damage control. Closed and secure WhatsApp groups allow consumers to speak to one another about a brand without participation by the brand. The saying, 'News travels fast, bad news travels faster' has never been truer: adverse brand news can reach millions in minutes.

Today, information and opinions about a brand are controlled less by the brand itself and more by its audiences. Many brands fight to stay in control. They try to hide adverse comments and complaints. They put out a barrage of counter-information. They respond to criticism through prepared statements. They use experts and influencers to bolster their credentials. But any brand taking a heavy-handed 'us against them' approach is swimming against the tide and refusing to accept that circumstances have changed for good. Such brands are likely to spend their marketing money in an unrewarding manner and tire themselves out, if not sink in exhaustion. Indian mobile phone brands are examples of this tendency, including the one-time powerhouse Micromax. As customer complaints about quality and service started to mount, many Indian mobile phone brands, instead of solving the problems with better products and more service centres, launched new models and expensive advertising campaigns. This only served to accentuate the swell of customer negativity, making it an easy hunting ground for the Chinese brands that have decimated Indian brands.

A more appropriate approach to brand information management today is 'us with them'. Brands must accept that the pendulum has swung irrevocably to the other side. Unprecedented power now lies with customers, special interest groups, NGOs, regulators and a range of other audiences. Brands must work *with* them, listening to their points of view, finding out how to make them allies, finding ways to have them volunteer positive reviews of the brand. Most importantly, a brand's information strategy has to change. It must no longer be about what the brand wants to say about itself (while hiding all the bad bits); it should be about what fires the interest and imagination of external audiences, so that they are at least neutral or mildly positive about a brand, or better still, openly admiring.

Knowledge of a brand is necessary but insufficient to get customers to engage with the brand further. This is why *awareness*, the first rung of the long-serving AIDA (awareness, interest, desire, action) model of advertising falls short of painting the complete picture. Awareness is necessary for all marketing of course, but awareness does not in itself create *engagement* with brands. Knowledge needs to combine with *relevance* to create *engagement*.

Think of engagement as that lean-forward moment when consumers go, 'Aha, this is something I have a place for in my world.' This happens organically, often at a category level, when consumers look for products and services in the natural rhythm of their lives. They are looking to go on a holiday, and voila!—all destination, travel agency, aggregator, hospitality, airline and other travel industry brands suddenly become relevant. After they return from the holiday, those brands fade into the background, until next time. When someone is looking for a new car, a school for a five-year-old, a restaurant to celebrate a special occasion or a fitted kitchen, the brands in each of those categories come into focus for a duration of time.

What do you do when you're not one of the brands fortunate enough to have an organic or periodic entry into consumers' lives? You have to work harder on relevance. As long as mutual funds relied primarily on occasional brand advertising and personal financial advisers to market them, the category had low penetration into the massive savings market in India. This started to change when these brands got together to form an industry association and, in 2016, launched a massive campaign to create relevance for the category. The campaign targeted the middle class, who ordinarily save their hard-earned rupees in bank deposits. It systematically overcame a range of knowledge and attitudinal barriers to create relevance and engagement for mutual funds. The results are outstanding, with many thousands of crores of rupees being invested in various mutual fund brands.

Feminine hygiene brands like Whisper and Stayfree have been in India for decades. Notwithstanding their efforts and some measure of success, sanitary pad penetration into the rural market remains low. Sankalp, an initiative by the Scindia Kanya Vidyalaya (SKV), Gwalior is a brilliant example of not just creating relevance for sanitary napkins among rural women but also inventing a business in the process. An enterprising group of school students provides a story large multinational brands can learn from.

Research conducted by SKV's students among women living in villages and slums revealed multiple challenges: low awareness of feminine hygiene and sanitary napkins; the impossibility of buying expensive branded sanitary napkins due to poverty; how social traditions made speaking openly about periods a taboo. Consequently, rural and slum women relied on unhygienic substitutes of sanitary pads, like cloth rags, during their periods.

Guided by their school principal, the students took a multipronged approach to solving the problem. They identified a small village near Gwalior called Zagra as a target for their transformative model and as a prototype for future expansion to other villages. Their goal was to provide the 250 women of Zagra with an uninterrupted supply of affordable sanitary napkins. They approached the famous 'Padman', Arunachalam Muruganatham of Jayaashree Industries, Coimbatore, and identified a machine to buy, one that used biodegradable materials like banana fibre to make low-cost sanitary napkins. Funds were raised through fairs, house sales and contributions from alumni and other donors. The machine arrived in the school and was installed. Training on how to use the machine was imparted to a pioneering group of staff and students. Other students, including boys from neighbouring schools, contributed their time and energy to the manufacturing of napkins. Soon, batches of napkins were ready for distribution. The distribution drives were accompanied by street skits performed by students, on themes confronting taboos and strictures, such as older women's horror of having menstruation spoken about in public, and provided information to Zagra's women on how to use the pads. The programme was soon a huge success. As pad usage grew, a machine was installed in Zagra, and the village women themselves were trained to manufacture pads, not just for their own use but as a business to earn income from—by supplying to women like themselves in other villages.

What a fabulous example of creating relevance and engagement! Incidentally, Sankalp is also a fabulous example of what the innovation guru Vijay Govindarajan, of Dartmouth College's Tuck School of Business, calls 'reverse innovation'.

But *engagement* itself does not create *preference*, especially in multiplayer categories. That 'lean-forward moment' described earlier in this chapter is vital but won't in itself create a unique brand connection. That's because any category's basic attributes and benefits are provided by most, if not all, the players. To transform engagement into preference, *differentiation* is the key. One has to look no further than India's telecom category for an example. By the mid-'90s, the unrepented multi-decade failure of public-sector companies to meet India's demand for phone services had created a ready-made market for mobile phone companies. Soon Airtel, Idea and Vodafone (and a few other early movers like Spice, Aircel and Reliance) had carved out the country among themselves, sharing several hundreds of millions of customers. Fast forward to the mid-2010s, when the category first expanded by upwards of fourteen players, including Telenor and Reliance, and later contracted to essentially three players—Airtel, Idea and Vodafone. With close to 70 per cent of the revenue market share between them, they also enjoyed a dominant profit share of the market. By 2013, it was widely known that Jio would enter the market, and while some apprehension was indeed felt by the three major players, they largely continued with business as usual.

Does this failure on the part of the three leading telecom brands to take anticipatory action present an uncomfortable parallel with Mirza Sajjad Ali, the character played by Sanjeev Kumar in Satyajit Ray's celebrated 1977 film *Shatranj Ke Khilari*? Mirza, when warned of the imminent arrival of British troops for the annexation of Awadh, is fatuously indolent. He is dismissive of the threat and returns to the attractions of the ongoing chess game with his long term friend and opponent Mir Raushan Ali, played by Saeed Jaffrey.

Regardless of whether the unflattering parallel with the annexation of Awadh is fair and applicable, Airtel, Idea and Vodafone chose not to pursue noticeable defensive differentiation, and in 2016 Jio marched in with rock-bottom pricing on data plans and free voice calls, pulling the rug from under the three established players. A brief three years later, in February 2019, the long-standing market leader Airtel was pushed to the third place with 301 million subscribers; Jio was, amazingly, already in the second place with 306 million subscribers; and Idea-Vodafone was first, with 387 million subscribers, principally on account of their merger. By mid-2020, the Idea-Vodafone combined entity is struggling to survive, and while Airtel is holding up, Jio is the brand to watch, the market differentiator and disruptor, the main game in town, consigning the older players, who aspire to match Jio's tactics, to the follower status.

When you add *differentiation* to *engagement*, you get *preference*.

But preference alone does not precipitate *brand desire*. There is one more thing that's needed: *brand esteem*. Esteem matters because all things being equal, even with preference created for a brand, if a final decision has to be made between two equally preferred choices, most consumers will pick the brand which they hold in greater esteem. The Body Shop, an international cosmetics brand, did a magnificent job of creating esteem in the Anita Roddick years. Their products had strong relevance across a range of categories and strong differentiation through a variety of natural ingredients, but what took the brand to very high esteem with consumers was The Body Shop's rejection of animal testing, as also their rejection of the 'thin and underfed' look that sells so many beauty and fashion products. (Their slogan was, 'There are 3 billion women who do not look like supermodels and only eight who do.')

Dove is another brand which wins esteem in a similar way. It talks of 'real beauty', features real women (wrinkles, scars, plus-sizes and all) and communicates without any artifice in a unique voice. Dove also has a 'Self-Esteem Project', to help women realize their dreams and ambitions, thereby raising Dove's own esteem among women.

With these components of the 'formula' falling into place through a well-orchestrated strategy, a brand is on the home stretch to forging a connection with customers. But *desire* in itself does not complete the puzzle; it does not translate into *demand* for the brand in the commercial sense. Desire married to dollars—or rupees, or pounds, or yen—equals demand. While it is great to have a demand for a brand, if customers don't have the means to acquire its products, the demand does not translate into sales. *Pricing*, or better still *affordability*, is the final piece that completes the brand connection jigsaw. That pricing is a key marketing mix variable is well-understood: apart from helping brands cover costs and make a profit, it communicates ideas about a brand's quality, craftsmanship, aesthetics, design, sophistication, aspiration and even elitism. The top fashion labels of the world have long made a science of pricing, as have a host of luxury brands. But even if you don't go that high, most categories have one or more high-quality, high-price players. In cars there are Mercedes-Benz, Audi and BMW; in detergents Ariel and Surf; in hotels the Taj and Grand Hyatt; in wristwatches Montblanc and Patek Philippe, and so on. Occasional price drops temporarily broaden the affordability of such brands and services and create demand. Loyalty schemes reward users with small and large additional benefits. These must be viewed differently from low-cost players offering tactical discounts. When SpiceJet or Go Air announce a lower fare offer, they are looking to ensure they have a full flight on a future date by incentivizing the confirmation of demand on an earlier date. This is different from when Mini, which sits in the luxury car segment in India, offers a special discount plus other benefits to make their car an attractive option for aspiring customers just off the range of their usual pricing.

So there you have it. This is the formula to create that very special thing every brand must have with its consumers: a connection.

Sustained brand connection is vital because the business landscape can be as harsh and inhospitable to brands as the Rub' al-Khali, the largest unbroken sand desert in the world, is to people wanting to cross it.

The Rub' al-Khali, or the 'empty quarter' in English, stretches for over 6,50,000 square kilometres across swathes of Saudi Arabia, Oman, the UAE and Yemen. The landscape is bleak and waterless. Commercial flights are routed around the Rub' al-Khali, for should an aircraft go down there, it would be impossible for rescuers to reach it. And yet, life exists in this wasteland. There are some places here that are considered good for grazing, and animal species, like the Arabian oryx and ostrich among others, have been known to exist in the region. In other words, life can thrive in the most seemingly harsh conditions once it establishes a connection with the topography. So too, in their world, can brands thrive when they establish connections with their audiences.

Forming a great brand connection is more than responding to a formula. It requires the skill to create, nurture and grow relationships. To make a brand relationship thrive is an art. We'll look at that in the next chapter.

IX

How to Build Thriving Relationships

Nugget 9: Customer Relationship Management Model

'Talk to me
Like lovers do
Walk with me
Like lovers do . . .'

—From the song 'Here Comes the Rain Again', by
Eurythmics

In this final chapter, I'm going to introduce you to two
models, which together will provide you with a framework
for understanding customer behaviour, so that you can use
that understanding to create actions that endear your brand
to customers.

The first model clusters customers into four boxes, by
comparing levels of satisfaction with a brand on the Y-axis
with the risk customers face in changing that brand on the
X-axis. This is a model I came across several years ago. I can't

any more remember where I came across it and therefore can't credit it accurately to its original authors, much as I would like to. What's more, I have made a few changes to the model I remember seeing all those years ago, so it resembles the anonymous original but is not a replica. I acknowledge my debt of gratitude to the original creators of the model, which I have found very useful in my work.

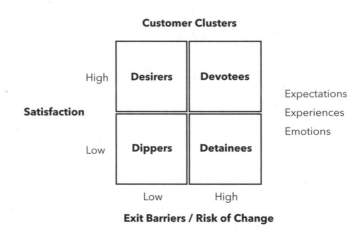

Let's look at the boxes as they would apply to the category of, say, ice cream. A further condition here is that we are only looking at such customers who have a dominant preference for ice cream over all other desserts. Unilever has a brand called Magnum, a part of their Wall's ice cream range. It is a largish chocolate-coated vanilla ice cream on a stick. The crisp, flaky chocolate coating is embellished with almonds in one variant and with dark chocolate in another; the vanilla core is replaced with sumptuous chocolate in the double-chocolate variant. Despite the variety within its range, at its core Magnum is a chocolate-coated vanilla stick. Magnum's marketing presents it as an immersive experience for the eater, typically shown as an attractive young woman. The woman's pleasure in eating Magnum has deliberate erotic insinuations, and the combination of product and imagery makes for a very attractive and successful ice cream. Priced higher than average sticks, Magnum is one of the more premium offerings in Unilever's ice cream catalogue.

Now suppose you are someone who tries a Magnum, and for some reason you are not blown away by the experience. It's not that you don't like it, but you realize that for you personally it is not all it's cracked up to be. Magnum has failed to enchant you in the manner it seems to enchant others. This might leave you open to another Magnum, or a Magnum variant, but you certainly aren't someone who has found the Magnum experience so delightful that nothing else will do. You might even be open to trying another brand instead of Wall's. If this is the case, you are a typical 'bottom-left box customer': your satisfaction is low, and your risk of change is low too. You are a 'dipper', someone who might buy a Magnum once in a while, alongside trying other ice creams as well. Your bond to Magnum is weak and does not prevent category promiscuity.

Now let's say you are someone who tries a Magnum, maybe the almond variant, and finds the experience delightful in every way. You love the rich chocolate coating crumbling under your tongue. You enjoy the crunch of the almonds against the smooth texture of the vanilla. You savour the Magnum until the last lick and feel ever so slightly disappointed when it's over. You feel the joy of discovering a brand that really appeals to you. Soon, Magnum is your first

choice of ice cream. You are a typical 'top-left box customer':
your satisfaction is high and you will likely not have another
ice cream if Magnum is available. You are a 'desirer', someone
who is highly satisfied with a brand and who chooses to give
time, attention and engagement to that brand even when the
cost of choosing a different brand is *not* high.

I am reminded of an experience when we lived in Dubai.
My wife, Michelle, and I had a weekly tradition of going to
the latest Friday movie release with another couple, friends
of ours. An unbreakable habit for us was a Magnum Almond
each at every movie. (And in more hedonistic moods,
even two!) We were out-and-out 'desirers'. Over time, our
enjoyment of Magnum Almond reached such heights that
if Magnum Almond was not available in the freezer at the
movie hall, we would, with great reluctance, accept another
Magnum variant. If every kind of Magnum was sold out *we
would do without ice cream,* but under no circumstances
would we settle for another Wall's brand or indeed another
brand's chocolate-vanilla stick. We had transitioned from the
top-left box into the top-right box: we had become Magnum
Almond 'devotees'. We had come to relish our brand to
such a degree that we would forego the entire category if our
brand was unavailable. We were so highly satisfied that we
created our own 'exit barriers'.

Customers in the final box, bottom-right, are 'detainees'.
These are customers who would ideally like to leave a brand
but are held there by factors other than free choice. In the
Magnum example, there are few reasons for customers to be
detainees, because the exit barrier/cost of change is not high
in ice cream. Customers will become Magnum detainees if,

hypothetically, every ice cream freezer in the city only sells Magnum. If this were the case, customers are left with no alternative but to have Magnum if they want an ice cream. Customers held hostage by a brand on account of supply will sooner or later take steps to overcome this. In the Magnum example, such steps may include choosing not to buy ice cream at all—leading to category attrition. Another example of brand detainees are air travellers from Bangkok to Koh Samui in Thailand. The only airline serving this sector is Bangkok Airways, and so, if you wish to fly from Bangkok to the island of Samui, you have to fly Bangkok Airways, accepting their prices, their timetable and their services. This is true for some aviation routes in India as well: from Delhi to Dharamsala, for example, you can fly either SpiceJet or Air India, and you must pay a premium for either.

A better Indian example of brand detainees comes from the mobile phone category of some years ago. In India, your mobile phone number is required to be on record for a large number of government and non-government services. For government services, it is attached to PAN cards, Aadhaar cards, income tax and GST return filings, railway bookings, cooking gas connections and a range of services and entitlements. In non-government areas, banking services, entertainment tickets, e-commerce maintenance contracts and various service alerts are attached to your mobile phone number. It is not unreasonable to say that in present-day India, our mobile numbers are a crucial first-level identity and gateway to services. For someone who extensively uses digital services, it used to be a massive burden, if not impossible, to change a mobile number of long standing, because of the number of individual service providers you had to update about your new number. Even if the services of the telecom company you used were not satisfactory—perhaps their network wasn't good, or the Internet data speeds were low, or the bills were too high— you couldn't shift to another, since you had registered your mobile number with so many service providers, which was a huge disincentive to change. You were a hostage of your mobile services provider because your exit barriers were too high. You were, in this case, a classic brand detainee: someone whose satisfaction levels are low but who continues to use a suboptimal service because exit barriers are too high. Fortunately, mobile number portability (MNP) has solved this problem in today's times. If you are unhappy with your provider, you can simply port out to another with no change in your number.

Every category, and every brand within a category, creates and manages *the three E's*: expectations, experiences and emotions. The performance of competing brands against the three E's impacts customer satisfaction, customer attitudes to exit barriers and brand switching. Customers have expectations from entire categories as well as from individual brands within each category. Their expectations touch upon two sides of the Brand Octagon: *performance* (the tangible benefits the brand will provide as a product and/or service), and *personality* (how the brand presents itself and what it says about the customers who use it).

Experiences have to do with actual brand interactions, events and outcomes. Experiences are where the promises brands make are delivered, or not delivered. Experiences are *moments of truth*, occasions when deep and lasting impressions are formed about brands. Moments of truth should be *moments of magic*, when the experience the brand delivers meets or exceeds expectations, making customers happy with, and positively disposed towards, the brand. But moments of truth could become *moments of misery*, if the brand experience falls so short of expectations that customers are left angry and dissatisfied.

I would like to tell a story about an experience I had with the American carrier Northwest Airlines at their hub in Detroit, USA. I was then based in Dubai, working with Lowe & Partners. ACDelco, a division of General Motors, was a client we looked after in the Gulf, on behalf of our partner, the Interpublic Group agency Campbell Ewald, based in Southfield, Michigan. Every November, I would make a short visit to Campbell Ewald, to go over various aspects of the business and professional relationship with our colleagues there. At the end of one such visit, I was checking in for my return Northwest flight at Detroit airport when I witnessed an event involving another passenger, a stranger to me. As all fliers know, check-in is a key moment of truth in airline travel: every passenger wants it to be at the very least smooth and problem-free, but better still so rewarding that it becomes a moment of magic. At the counter next to mine, a passenger had come to check in for his flight and was being told that, despite the two previous cancellations of his onward journey by Northwest (as a consequence of which the passenger had spent many hours waiting at the airport), he was going to have to wait several more hours before being put on a flight that would arrive at his destination via another city! The passenger, clearly tired and upset, lost his patience and raised his voice in protest. Tempers surged on both sides of the counter and soon, the counter staff summoned security. Two large security personnel arrived and, sandwiching the unfortunate passenger between them, frogmarched him away. A disturbed hush fell over the check-in area. All passengers, including me, even though I'd actually had a smooth and trouble-free check-in at the adjacent counter, were terribly unsettled by that poor passenger's plight. If there was ever a moment of truth that had become a moment of misery, this was it. Despite the fact that the incident had not happened to me personally, I was so adversely affected by it that I never flew Northwest Airlines again. Such is the power of experience; such is the power of a moment of truth.

Obviously, every brand aspires to multiple moments of magic and zero, or at least as few as possible, moments of misery. The more successful brands realize this aspiration consistently.

The third E—emotions—has to do with how people feel before, during and after using a brand. Take the example of a beautiful woman, now in her mid-forties, who is concerned about the lines the passing years have put around her eyes. She is persuaded by the promise of a firming gel that makes the skin around the eyes tighter, reducing the appearance of wrinkles, in just fourteen days. The woman buys the brand's firming gel and, lo and behold, she finds the promise to be true: the wrinkles around her eyes have visibly reduced in fourteen days, just as the brand had claimed. How does this make her feel? On the human level, younger and more beautiful. At the brand level, a believer. In the language of the Customer Clusters model, she goes from being a 'dipper' to a 'desirer'. The brand has put the customer in an emotionally happier place: she has reversed time to see a younger version of herself and possibly decreased her perceived rate of ageing. If 'expectations' are about functionality and performance, 'emotions' are about feelings, and 'experiences' bridge both functionality and feelings. As the famous saying goes, 'They may forget what you said, they may forget what you did, but they will never forget how you made them feel.'

Every brand's customer base distributes across the four boxes: dippers, desirers, devotees and detainees. And each set of customers behaves differently when it comes to their responses to brands based on the three E's. As a general rule, customers are less likely to express satisfaction publicly and more likely to take to social media to air dissatisfaction. Dippers are also less likely to publicly voice brand opinions than devotees and detainees, albeit the latter two for very different reasons. Needless to say, it is in every brand's interest to maximize the number of desirers and devotees and eliminate or minimize the number of detainees.

Dippers often speak of brands as one of many choices. Here's an example: let's say we are a packaged breakfast cereal company speaking to a group of Indian mothers, with children below ten years of age, on the subject of breakfast. The moms will unsurprisingly be voluble and opinionated; we will indubitably hear about a range of expectations, experiences and emotions to do with breakfast. The moms will share their stories about the challenges they face trying to get a healthy breakfast into their children every morning against the pressures of time. They will speak of poor eaters and good eaters; of children who resist breakfast; of the need for variety to keep breakfast interesting. They will share the challenge of taste vs goodness; of the temptation to offer a dish that goes down easily but isn't very nutritious vs something that is good for health but a struggle to get their children to eat. They will speak of traditional Indian hot breakfasts on the one hand and, on the other, of eggs, toast, packaged meats and breakfast cereals. They will tell us what children like and don't like, and where, if at all, a breakfast cereal might fit. Beyond the specifics of breakfast, they will speak about their anxieties regarding their children not eating well, but also about their hopes that their children do well in life, both in the present and in the future. It's not easy being a mom at any time, and breakfast could be one of parenting's many stresses. Somewhere, in that mass of words, they will give us clues as to their expectations, experiences and emotions in relation to the range of choices in the breakfast category, including our breakfast cereal brand. And we, the breakfast cereal company, must make these clues the basis of a marketing strategy that converts the moms first into dippers, then desirers and finally devotees of our brand.

Sure enough, categories show differences in customer behaviour, based on satisfaction drivers and the scales of exit barriers. Small-investment, modest-expectation, low-exit-barrier categories like biscuits, chocolates, bathing soap and agarbattis are likely to demonstrate one kind of customer behaviour, with many more dippers than desirers and devotees, and very few, if any, detainees. As customers' expectations from categories rise and their experiences and emotions vary, often with a commensurate decrease in the flexibility to change to another brand, they start to dip less and invest more time in pre-purchase decision-making. If one is buying a new car, or having one's home painted, the outlay is large and the interval between purchases in the region of five years. Exit barriers are high, cost of change is high, satisfaction demanded is high. The expectations, experiences and emotions quotient of such categories is different from that of the less expensive, frequent-consumption categories and brands. When you think of schools as a category, the interval may be, well . . . never: a student may enter school and leave for college only after finishing the twelfth and final grade. The consequences of making a wrong choice of school can be crushing, and therefore parents choose schools very carefully. But despite this, school brands tend to have a high proportion of detainees—parents who voice their dissatisfaction to other parents and on social media about a range of personal irritants and concerns.

Every brand would like a high percentage of desirers and devotees and a very small percentage of dippers and detainees. It makes brands more resilient to new entries, business more predictable, word-of-mouth publicity more effective and attracts loyalty as well as new users. How does a brand make this happen? The answer lies in the following customer relationship management model.

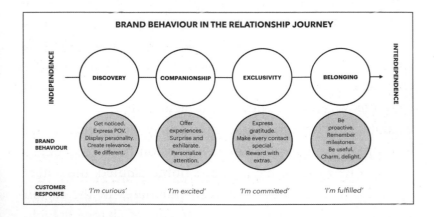

The journey a successful human relationship makes has long served as an analogy for the brand-consumer relationship journey. It's an accurate and useful analogy, especially for brands that aspire to managing their customer clusters well.

The starting point of the journey is 'independence' and the end point is 'interdependence'. In human relationships, independence could mean being happily single, perhaps going on dates, but not wanting anything more. In brand terms, independence is a state where a customer is enjoying a stable and largely satisfying experience from a set of brands and therefore not in active search of something new. Interdependence is the state where both parties have acknowledged and embraced the symbiotic role each has in creating and maintaining mutual fulfilment. In brand terms, this means a brand making a central, integral and 'counted-upon' place for itself in a customer's life.

There are four stages in the journey from independence to interdependence: discovery, companionship, exclusivity and belonging. Let's explore the four stages using human relationships as the landscape and a fictitious couple, Abhay and Maia, as lead characters. Like many young professionals, their careers have brought them to Mumbai. Abhay is in his late twenties, has a great job, a nice sense of style, is articulate, well-read, interesting and a thoughtful and considerate person. Abhay meets Maia through common friends and is instantly attracted to her. Maia, also in her twenties possessing many of the lovely attributes that Abhay personifies and some very attractive ones of her own, runs into Abhay often at overlapping events. She is friendly and accessible but has never shown evidence of wanting to know

Abhay on closer terms. Yet Abhay feels that Maia is not uninterested. He aspires to move himself and Maia from a state of independence, where each is stable in their current relationship status, to a state of interdependence, where they will have intertwined lives, incomplete without the other's presence in it. What must Abhay do to move this relationship from friendship to something more?

The five points in the first circle of the relational management model, under 'discovery', indicate the first set of actions Abhay must take. The five points are: get noticed, express a point of view, display personality, create relevance and be different. For Maia to look at Abhay as a potential partner, Abhay must stand out from all the other young men in their friend circle. To do so, Abhay can't be invisible or too accommodative, he has to display his personality and express provocative points of view. Express provocative points of view about what? About the things Maia finds relevant, the things she finds interesting and likes spending time on. But relevance and common ground, while crucial, are not enough. Abhay can't be someone who simply agrees with Maia and the others at all times and on most things. He has to offer a unique perspective on topics of common interest. In doing so, he will, in time, become someone whose unusual take on things Maia finds engaging and looks forward to. Her reaction: 'Abhay is clearly a very interesting guy. I'm curious about him.' So Abhay has been 'discovered' and is on his way with Maia!

In the second stage—companionship—Abhay and Maia will spend one-on-one time with each other, exploring common interests and deepening their understanding and appreciation of each other. But this does not mean Abhay is the only person Maia is spending time with. She will be going out with other people, among them other potential interdependence partners. For Abhay to negotiate the companionship stage successfully, he will have to offer experiences Maia can't get elsewhere. He will have to surprise and exhilarate her, he will have to personalize and customize contact with her. Companionship is a very important phase in the journey, as Maia is seeking and storing information through every interaction about her compatibility with Abhay and his suitability as a partner. More than the rational aspects of Abhay's qualities, Maia will also be mining every event for emotional clues to Abhay's worthiness as a partner. If all goes well, she would not just say to herself, 'Abhay is comfortable to be with; he is suitable.' Instead, she would say something more thrilling than that. She would say to herself, 'I'm excited to be with him.'

With the companionship phase successfully negotiated, Abhay proposes the third phase—exclusivity. Maia feels the same way. And so, both of them commit to exclusivity, to be a couple. They choose to forego other potential partners. They choose to spend as much time together as they can. They may even choose to give up living independently and move in together. Romantic comedies, perhaps wisely, are careful to end their stories when a couple commits to each other, because *exclusivity marks the beginning of the most difficult phase in the relationship journey.*

Exclusivity will make many demands on Maia and Abhay, as both give everything to their relationship. This will place considerable pressure on them both and often stretch their feelings for each other to breaking point. For Abhay and Maia to navigate the exclusivity stage of the relationship journey successfully, the three points in the relationship management model corresponding to this stage provide the road map: Abhay must express gratitude to Maia for her presence in his world (flowers, cards, phone calls); second, he must make their moments together special and memorable (tickets to that impossible-to-get-tickets-for show Maia has always wanted to see; remembering to carry an umbrella on a rainy day because she won't); and third, he must make sure he brings unsolicited extras to their time together (favourite chocolate, just-right coffee, a potted plant for her window nook, a new book by that author she loves). Assuming it is an equal relationship, Maia too will have to do similar things for Abhay.

And in time, with exclusivity well established, Maia is in the belonging stage. She likes where she's at: in life and with Abhay. In her thoughts, she says, 'I'm fulfilled.' But it's not like Abhay can now stop making an effort. For belonging not to backslide into earlier stages of the relationship journey, Abhay must take the actions suggested in the circle below 'belonging' in my model. Abhay must make proactive contact (call Maia at work during the day to see how she's getting along), broaden the conversation with Maia to expand their areas of mutual interest, remember milestones (anniversaries and birthdays being the bare minimum), be of use (yes, Abhay will speed-post Maia's income tax filing) and charm and delight (her, as well as her friends and family).

Thus, Abhay and Maia navigate the relationship journey from independence to interdependence with a happy outcome.

As with human relationships, so it is with brands.

As someone famously said, 'It is better to be noticed once than ignored twice.' Few things describe brand behaviour in the discovery phase better than this provocative comment. Customers are subject to the triple barriers of attention, apathy and time. To overcome these barriers, brands must do all it takes to be noticed. One powerful way to get noticed is to express a unique and relevant point of view, not just on the product category but on life itself. Tata Tea's 'Jaago Re' campaign is one such unique and relevant point of view. Brands must demonstrate a striking personality and create relevance for themselves in relation to the consumers. Pepperfry, the online furniture store, does a good job of this. In the previous chapter, we looked at the importance of relevance in the formula for brand connection. Discovery is a key phase for creating relevance. The customer response when this is done well is typically, 'I'm curious,' signifying that the brand has garnered attention in a positive manner.

Companionship is a stage that many brands ignore in their rush to complete a commercial transaction. Brands that don't make this mistake and offer surprising, delightful and as far as possible personalized experiences elicit the response, 'I'm excited.' They gain something of immeasurable value in a relationship: time spent with the brand. Customers in the companionship stage transact with a brand but they could well be with other brands at the same time. For example, prepaid customers in the mobile phone market who hold multiple SIM cards.

The companionship phase could be long or short depending on the category. As a rule, the higher the customer's investment in a category, the deeper the investigation he or she carries out about competing brands, and the longer the duration of companionship. In the automobile market, companionship can be prolonged. Having put down certain specifications—like budget, type of car, colour and desired features—customers will visit a range of brand showrooms, car comparison sites, view videos of expert drive tests, read reviews by owners, and ask friends and family for their opinions. Only then would customers book a particular brand and model.

Exclusivity does not necessarily mean the customer is deliriously happy and will remain in a state of perpetual happiness. It means that a customer has chosen to give business to a brand—*but it equally means that the customer has transferred all expectations from the category on to that brand.* It is a challenging stage of the relationship but an important one, especially for those interested in lifetime customer value. That's why unboxing and onboarding are vital steps of the exclusivity phase. I have heard horror stories of parts found missing during the unboxing of a product, and of hidden costs being applied by certain brands. Many domestic appliances brands in India do a very poor job of onboarding, taking several more days to install than they promise, despite receiving full payment in advance. Brands that express gratitude and reward customers with extras get the very welcome response, 'I'm committed.' Brands that don't do this typically give customers problems from day one of exclusivity, with customers feeling let down just when they should be feeling thrilled. Customers should be going from the desirers box into the devotees box during exclusivity. It is worth remembering that the brand is still under assessment in many ways during exclusivity, and should a brand fail to change desirers into devotees, they may quickly become detainees.

Brand-consumer interdependence is manifest in its fullest in the belonging stage. This is when the relationship is at its fulfilled best for both sides. Many hotels have high-end customers who stay exclusively with them in an expression of the consumer mindset, 'I'm fulfilled.' In terms of domestic appliances, this is where post-purchase service kicks in in a big way. Customers of brands with weak, poor-quality or overpriced service rapidly deteriorate into detainees. Those who are well looked after in terms of service become desirers and devotees.

Easy though this journey is to talk about, it is very hard to walk the talk. Unlike the relationship between Maia and Abhay, brand-customer relationships are unequal, with brands having to do all the heavy lifting to keep the relationship alive and healthy. Customer promiscuity is legendary. They will move on quickly and ruthlessly when something new comes along or when their needs change. Brands have to be ever vigilant and nimble-footed to keep their relationships relevant and refreshed, or suffer the fate of Kodak and Nokia.

Epilogue: The Busy Person's Summary

Here's a 'ready reckoner' to help you quickly access the ideas in this book. A regular glance at it, together with a detailed immersion in the book when called for, will help you create an exceptional marketing strategy for your brand, based on the solid foundation of customer concept.

Section 1: How to Think of People

Nugget 1: *Who Are We Talking To?*

The Multi-Identity Customer Is Now Mainstream

Step past the beguiling homogeneity of single-identity customers. Customers have always been multi-identity, and today they unabashedly express the diverse aspects of their individuality. For modern-day marketing, this is an opportunity and a challenge. Marketers who embrace the idea of multiple-identity customers will help their brands respond better to present-day challenges and opportunities.

Nugget 2: Why Do People Buy?

A New Customer Motivation Model

People buy in response to their needs and motivators. My model organizes customer motivation into seven outward-directed motivators and seven inward-directed motivators. The seven outward-directed motivators are one-upmanship, FOMO (fear of missing out), attention, connection, vanity, social credit and public legacy. The seven inward-directed motivators are good sense, self-love, hedonism, joy of ownership, personal reinvention, value-added experiences and private legacy. These motivators are in constant churn within each of us, singly or in conjunction with one another, creating the impulse to buy. The motivators have four influencers: money, values, personality and time.

Nugget 3: How Do We Influence People?

Uses of the Customer Motivation Model

While there are many uses of the model, three that stand out are:

1) For the integration of business goals and marketing strategy. Simply put: there is no business without customers; there is no customer without marketing; great

marketing is about building great brands; great brands make and keep more customers.

2) For value-added customer segmentation. Demographic segmentation models are useful but have limitations. My motivators-based model leads to more meaningful segmentation, unconfined by the typical variables, such as gender, age and geography.

3) For product and brand development. The fourteen motivators lead marketers to better differentiated products and brands.

Section 2: How to Craft Your Brand

Nugget 4: Where Do Brands Come From?

Learning from the Past to Shape Tomorrow's Brands

Brands have a long history, reaching back in time all the way to cavemen. Over the centuries, brands have evolved in step with societies and new ways of life. Delving into the history of brands gives important clues as to where brands have come from and where they are going.

Nugget 5: How Did Brands Get Here?

From Brand Positioning to Brand Authenticity, and the Brand Octagon Model for the Twenty-First-Century Brand

Over a century ago, brands were commodities with names. Then came a range of sophistications, answering to the specific needs of each era. Brand positioning, brand idea, brand ideal and brand purpose have all had their day. In the 2020s, brand authenticity is of paramount importance.

My Brand Octagon model helps marketers conceptualize authentic brands. The core of the Octagon is made up of the answers to three questions brands are asked: Why are you here? What do you do? How do you do it? The eight sides of the Octagon—performance, product interface, pricing, service, impact on planet, culture, storytelling and customer experience—bring depth and differentiation to your brand.

Nugget 6: Where Are Brands Going?

How to Craft an Authentic Brand

Two pools of brand DNA help marketers craft authentic brands. Each pool has eight strands. The 'Invisible DNA' pool consists of: history, vision, mission, purpose, values, people, culture and competencies. The 'Visible DNA' pool also has eight strands: product, packaging, pricing, presence, personality, visual identity, content and media. These are the identifiers that create and communicate authenticity to customers.

Section 3: How to Go to Market

Nugget 7: How to Talk to People

Creating Powerful Brand Content

A handy 'formula' for creating content is contained in the initialism ABCDE. A for attention (did you notice it?); B for branding (who was it from?); C for communication (what did it say?); D for decoding (what does that mean for you?); E for engagement (what does that make you feel and do?).

Marketers should also look at a five-point communication strategy:

1) Communicate across the entire customer journey
2) Make a comprehensive broadcast and narrowcast plan
3) Deploy the entire Brand Octagon in communication
4) Create a pipeline for superlative branded content
5) Measure performance and be nimble to change

Nugget 8: How to Create Strong Connections

The formula for brand connection is:

Contact + Information = Knowledge
Knowledge + Relevance = Engagement
Engagement + Differentiation = Preference
Preference + Esteem = Desire
Desire + Pricing = Demand

Nugget 9: How to Build Thriving Relationships?

Customer Relationship Management Model

Based on their expectations from, experiences with and emotions about brands, customers divide into four categories: dippers, desirers, devotees and detainees. By elevating moments of truth into moments of magic, brands can convert more of their customers into desirers and devotees.

To do this well, brands must manage all four stages of the customer journey—discovery, companionship, exclusivity and belonging—with panache and personality.

Remind yourselves of the nine nuggets frequently, if not every day. They will help you craft and execute a great marketing strategy. They will put you on the road to becoming a marketing legend. Bon voyage!

Acknowledgements

I owe a huge debt of gratitude to Arundhati Dasgupta, formerly of *Business Standard*, who saw a book in me and helped me give it shape; and to Radhika Marwah and Vineet Gill of Penguin Random House India, who took me under their wing and made me a better writer.

A first-time writer's journey has its share of ups and downs. *Nine Timeless Nuggets* wouldn't have been possible without my wife, Michelle, and children, Kunal and Divya, whose constant encouragement and good-natured wisecracks made the process enjoyable and took me over the odd bump in the road.

Finally, I would like to say a huge thank you to the many clients, colleagues, family and friends who, having heard I was doing this book, lavished me with their support and good wishes.

Mumbai   Bharat Bambawale
November 2020